ServSafe
National Restaurant Association

Record your class number here.

SERVSAFE ALCOHOL®

Fundamentals of Responsible Alcohol Service

SECOND EDITION

DISCLAIMER

Table of Contents

INTRODUCTION...ii

    A Message from the National Restaurant Association............ ii

    Acknowledgments...iii

    How to Use *Fundamentals of Responsible Alcohol Service* iv

CHAPTER 1: ALCOHOL LAW AND YOUR RESPONSIBILITY........1-1

    Your Responsibility as a Seller or Server of Alcohol 1-3

    The Role of the Liquor Authority 1-6

    Laws Restricting Alcohol Service 1-8

CHAPTER 2: RECOGNIZING AND PREVENTING INTOXICATION 2-1

    Alcohol and the Body..2-2

    Assessing a Guest's Level of Intoxication 2-8

    Preventing Guests from Becoming Intoxicated 2-19

CHAPTER 3: CHECKING IDENTIFICATION 3-1

    Acceptable Forms of Identification......................................3-4

    Verifying Identification...3-5

    When to Check IDs 3-13

    The Proper Procedure for Checking IDs 3-14

    Using ID Readers 3-16

    Dealing with a Fake ID 3-16

CHAPTER 4: HANDLING DIFFICULT SITUATIONS 4-1

    Handling Intoxicated Guests...4-2

    Handling Potentially Violent Situations...........................4-12

    Handling Illegal Activities...4-13

    Documenting Incidents...4-16

INDEX IN-1

CREDITS C-1

A MESSAGE FROM
The National Restaurant Association

The National Restaurant Association is pleased to bring you ServSafe Alcohol® *Fundamentals of Responsible Alcohol Service, Second Edition.*

Risk management is crucial to the success of every restaurant and foodservice operation. Serving alcohol responsibly is critical to preventing difficult circumstances in establishments and, ultimately, in the community. To develop these materials, we convened foodservice, regulatory, legal, academic, medical, and insurance experts to build a training program that focuses on what front-of-house employees need to know to serve alcohol responsibly.

By opening this book, you have made a significant commitment to responsible alcohol service. ServSafe Alcohol is designed to train all members of an establishment, including servers, hosts, valets, bouncers, coat checkers, etc. The program gives you information on understanding alcohol law and your responsibility, recognizing and preventing intoxication, checking identification, and handling difficult situations. You will also find places to record local laws and your company policies.

The Association is dedicated to helping you serve alcohol responsibly. Additional materials to help you learn and retain responsible alcohol practices include:

- **Videos and DVDs.** Throughout the training course, videos/DVDs bring classroom material into real-world situations. Four of the videos/DVDs correspond to a respective chapter of the text. A fifth video/DVD will help you see challenging real-world scenarios involving guests who might be intoxicated, ID checking, and employees handling difficult situations.

- **Training throughout the organization.** Front-of-house training is vital to responsible alcohol service. The next step is responsible alcohol management. The Association is currently creating training programs that reach all levels within an organization, which assist in creating consistent alcohol-management objectives.

We applaud you for making the commitment to serving alcohol responsibly. Your training is a beneficial step toward making your operation and your community safe. For more information on ServSafe Alcohol, please visit **www.ServSafe.com/alcohol.**

ACKNOWLEDGMENTS

The development of *Fundamentals of Responsible Alcohol Service* would not have been possible without the expertise of our many advisors, contributors, and manuscript reviewers. We are pleased to thank the following people for their time, effort, and dedication in creating the second edition of this book.

2009 I.D. Checking Guide
courtesy of The Drivers License Guide Company

Adam Balick
Law firm of Balick & Balick

Jan Byrne
Alabama Alcoholic Beverage Control Board

Jack Carey
Aramark Corporation / Allstate Arena

Suzanne Carpenter
Carlson Restaurants Worldwide

Dimitrios Christopoulos
Law firm of Wilcox & Christopoulos, LLC

Kat Cole
Hooters of America

Harry D'Ercole, Jr. and the staff of
Enrico's Italian Dining, Frankfort, IL

Keith Doerge
The Drivers License Guide Company

Pradeep Dudeja, Ph.D
University of Illinois at Chicago,
Department of Physiology in Medicine

Mary Anne Ferrell
Darden Restaurants

Derek Fournier
Uno Restaurant Corp.

Nikki Fuchs
Buffalo Wild Wings

Steve Garrett
Garrett Photography

Scott Gellar Ph.D
Virginia Polytechnic University
Center for Applied Behavior Systems

Tony Glavas and the staff of
The Courtyard Bistro, Frankfort, IL

Commander Tim Goergen
Bloomingdale, IL Police Department

Robert Gomez
Subterranean Nightclub

Ken Hirsch
CNA E&S Insurance

Vicki Houston
Damon's International

Roger Johnson
Wisconsin Department of Revenue,
Alcohol & Tobacco Enforcement Division

Brian Kringen
Minnesota Department of Public Safety

Kenneth and Jillian Kukla and the staff of
Jackson's Bar & Grill, St. John, IN

Lydia R. Menzel, Ed.D
Performance Partnership, Inc.

Jennifer Michaud
CHAMPPS

William Miller, Ph.D
University of New Mexico,
Department of Psychology

Ron Molk
Classic Images

Shalon Morris
Carlson Restaurants Worldwide / TGI Friday's

Ed Mugnani and the staff of
Café 200—AON Center Cafeteria

Alfred Rasho
Roxy Media Corporation

Lee Roupas
Illinois Liquor Control Commission

Kathy Rusnacko
Famous Dave's of America

Warren Sackler, CHA, FMP
Rochester Institute of Technology,
Hospitality and Service Management
Department

Chief Darrell Sanders, Ret.
Frankfort, IL Police Department

Christine San Juan
Bertucci's Corporation

Robert Schaefer
Bennigan's

Angie Simmons
CHAMPPS

Steve Skonecke and the staff of
Kansas Street Grill, Frankfort, IL

Michael Storm
Harrah's Casino, Joliet, IL

Traci Toomey, Ph.D
University of Minnesota,
School of Public Health

Rich and Sara Tucker
Product Evaluations, Inc.

James Webster
Law firm of Webster Powell

Viage ID reader
courtesy of CardCom Technology

HOW TO USE
Fundamentals of Responsible Alcohol Service

Suggested below is a plan for studying and retaining the responsible alcohol service knowledge in this textbook that is vital to protecting you, your guests, and your establishment.

Beginning Each Chapter

Prepare for the section by completing the following.

- **Review the learning objectives.** Located on the front page of each chapter, the learning objectives identify tasks you should be able to do after finishing the chapter. They are linked to the essential practices for serving alcohol responsibly.

- **Test your knowledge.** Before you begin reading, test your prior knowledge of some of the chapter's concepts by answering five True or False questions. If you want to explore the concepts behind the questions further, see the page references provided. Answers are located at the back of each chapter.

Throughout Each Section

Use these features to help you identify and reinforce the concepts in the chapter.

- **Concepts.** These topics are important for a thorough understanding of responsible alcohol service. They are identified before the introduction to each chapter.

- **Graphics.** Placed throughout each chapter to visually reinforce the key concepts in the text, they include charts, photographs, illustrations, and tables.

- **Something to Think About.** Based on real-world examples, these stories reveal the potential impact of careless alcohol service.

- **How This Relates to Me.** Throughout each chapter, you can write in information specific to your location or operation, such as alcohol-related laws or company policies. If you are training in a group, your instructor may provide this information; if you are training with your manager or studying independently, you should research these topics to ensure you have the most appropriate information for your jurisdiction.

- **Activities.** Apply what you have learned by completing the various activities throughout each chapter. In chapters 2, 3, and 4, you will have the opportunity to apply what you have learned by viewing and responding to scenes presented in a video/DVD corresponding to this text called *Evaluating Real-World Scenarios.* Answers for activities are located at the back of each chapter.

At the End of Each Section

Once you have finished reading and completing the activities throughout each chapter, see how well you have learned.

■ **Answer the multiple-choice study questions.** These questions are designed to test your knowledge of the concepts presented in the chapter. If you have difficulty answering them, you should review the content further. Answers are located at the back of each chapter.

1

Alcohol Law and Your Responsibility

After completing this chapter, you should be able to:

■ Identify criminal liability as it relates to the sale and service of alcohol.

■ Identify criminal violations related to the sale and service of alcohol and their consequences.

■ Identify civil liability as it relates to the sale and service of alcohol.

■ Define dram shop law.

■ Recognize the impact of employee violations on the owner and the establishment and identify consequences.

■ Identify the role of the liquor authority.

■ Identify liquor authority violations and their consequences.

■ Identify laws restricting alcohol service.

Note: The information provided is intended only to inform and assist the reader in understanding basic areas of alcohol law and the responsibilities involved therein. The information provided should not be considered legal advice, nor is it intended to address how particular laws may apply to a problem that might arise. The reader is encouraged to discuss any specific problem with appropriate counsel before making any decision with respect to the matters discussed or the information provided in this chapter.

TEST YOUR KNOWLEDGE

1. True or False: You may be charged with a crime simply for serving a guest who appears to be intoxicated. *(See page 1-4.)*

2. True or False: It is illegal to serve alcohol to a pregnant woman. *(See page 1-9.)*

3. True or False: Dram shop laws protect the server from being sued in the event that an intoxicated guest injures another individual. *(See page 1-4.)*

4. True or False: The state liquor authority can suspend an establishment's liquor license for allowing a minor to enter the establishment with a fake ID. *(See page 1-6.)*

5. True or False: All guests must be 21-years-old to purchase alcohol. *(See page 1-8.)*

For answers, please turn to page 1-12.

CONCEPTS

■ **Criminal liability:** Being held responsible for committing a crime. Servers can be held criminally liable for violating alcohol-service laws. These laws are often created and enforced by states, counties, cities, towns, and villages.

■ **Civil liability:** Being held responsible for payment of damages for injuring a person. Servers can be sued and forced to pay damages if their actions or lack of care while serving alcohol leads to an injury.

■ **Dram shop laws:** Laws that allow an establishment's owners and employees to be sued by someone injured by a guest who had been drinking alcohol at the establishment.

■ **Liquor authority:** State or municipal agency that enforces alcohol regulations and licensing laws.

■ **Municipality:** City, town, county, or village.

YOUR RESPONSIBILITY AS A SELLER OR SERVER OF ALCOHOL

As a member of the service staff, you must understand your liability regarding alcohol service. Being liable means you have legal responsibilities. If you break liquor laws, you could face:

- Law suits
- Criminal charges
- Fines
- Imprisonment
- Closure of your establishment

You must always balance the desire to please your guests with your legal responsibilities regarding alcohol service. Sometimes the customer is not always right. Serving alcohol responsibly will help you meet your legal responsibilities. It's also the right thing to do.

This chapter will give you a better understanding of general alcohol laws and how they directly affect you.

SOMETHING TO THINK ABOUT...

The following is based on a true story.

It was a busy Saturday evening at a club in a small Midwestern town. One of the establishment's regulars sat quietly at the bar. The bartender poured the man his favorite drink. As the night progressed, he kept an eye on the glass of his regular, ready for the man's signal to fill it again.

About two hours later, showing no signs of intoxication, the regular left. He got in his truck to drive the two miles from the club to his house. Five minutes after leaving the establishment, he crashed his truck into a car carrying two 20-year-old college students. All three were killed. In the subsequent investigation, it was discovered that the man had consumed a fifth of liquor in the two hours he was at the club, or the equivalent of 17 drinks.

In a civil suit brought by the students' parents, the owners of the club were ordered to pay $500,000 to the families. The establishment also lost its liquor license and was forced to close. In addition, the bartender was tried and convicted of criminal recklessness, and given the maximum penalty. He was ordered to serve 180 days in jail, as well as to pay a fine. Lastly, as a condition of his sentence, the judge ordered the bartender to place a picture of the deceased students in his jail cell for the length of his term.

Criminal Liability

As a seller or server of alcohol, you may face criminal charges if you break state, county, or municipal alcohol laws.

Most states may hold you criminally liable if you:

- Serve alcohol to a minor

- Serve a guest who is or appears to be intoxicated

- Possess, sell, or allow the sale of drugs on the premises

The consequences of these violations can be serious. Depending on the state in which you work, you could be placed on probation, fined, or even given jail time. In Florida, for example, selling or serving alcohol to a minor is punishable by a fine of $1,000 and a liquor-license suspension of seven days.

Civil Liability

You have a civil liability when selling or serving alcohol. This means that you can be sued and forced to pay damages to an injured guest if you contributed to the guest's injury or did nothing to prevent the injury.

Dram Shop Laws

Many states have passed dram shop laws. These laws create a special kind of civil liability for establishments and their employees. Dram shop laws:

- Allow a third party—who may not have been in the establishment— to sue for injuries caused by a guest who was drinking there.

- Allow third parties to sue the business, the business owner(s), and the employees.

- Provide "caps" (or limits) on money damages that can be awarded to third parties. These caps vary by state.

During any lawsuit, the court will look at the actions you took at the time of the incident. Most important, the court will try to determine if:

- You were the cause of the guest becoming intoxicated.

- Guests were allowed or even encouraged to become intoxicated in the establishment.

- Policies were in place to protect guests from overconsumption.

It is critical to serve alcohol responsibly to prevent injuries to guests and third parties.

SOMETHING TO THINK ABOUT...

The following are based on true stories.

Driving home from a party at a friend's house, a couple on their motorcycle was struck by an oncoming car. The man on the motorcycle broke every bone in his left leg, from foot to hip. His wife, seated behind him, suffered a severe pelvic injury, rendering her unable to have children.

Upon investigation, it was revealed that the driver of the car had recently left a private party at a local, casual-dining establishment. In civil court, the couple sued the restaurant for serving a guest who was visibly intoxicated. During the trial, a subpoenaed server testified that she knew the driver of the car had been drunk but had continued to serve him anyway. The jury found in favor of the couple, awarding them $39 million in damages.

In another case, a 25-year-old woman drove her car into a utility pole soon after leaving a small pub. According to the coroner's report, her BAC was twice the legal limit. Based on that information, the woman's family named the bar's owners and the bartender in a civil lawsuit, seeking over $25,000 in damages. It was subsequently revealed that at no point did the bar stop service to the woman, despite knowing she was driving home.

APPLY YOUR KNOWLEDGE: *List the Crime*

List three alcohol-law violations that most states will hold you criminally liable for.

1. Serving to a minor
2. Serving apears to be intoxicated
3. Possesion /selling /Knowledge of drugs on premises

For answers, please turn to page 1-12.

THE ROLE OF THE LIQUOR AUTHORITY

Each state has its own liquor laws. To complicate matters, many municipalities have their own, often stricter, laws. Each state and many municipalities have a liquor authority. These are often called the Alcoholic Beverage Control or Liquor Control Commission. These agencies are responsible for:

- Enforcing alcohol laws
- Issuing and monitoring liquor licenses
- Issuing citations for violations
- Holding hearings for violators of the liquor code

HOW THIS RELATES TO ME...

In my state/municipality, my liquor authority is

Getting a liquor license is not a right. It is a privilege granted to establishments that meet certain conditions. Citations can be issued to owners and employees if these conditions are violated.

The liquor authority can issue citations for:

- Selling liquor to a minor
- Failing to check the ID of a guest who appears to be underage
- Allowing a minor to enter the establishment with a fake ID
- Serving a guest who is or appears to be intoxicated
- Discriminating against guests due to race, gender, age, or sexual orientation
- Selling or serving alcohol when it is not permitted

A liquor authority violation can result in the suspension or revocation of the establishment's license.

These violations can result in a fine for the server and the owner. The establishment's liquor license can also be suspended or revoked, which can put it out of business. In states that license servers to serve alcohol, the state may also take away the server's license.

Law enforcement and agents from the liquor authority can visit your establishment at any time. Always be polite when you greet them. Then notify your manager.

Cooperate when law enforcement enters your establishment.

SOMETHING TO THINK ABOUT...

Compliance checks, or stings, are a common way for the liquor authority and local law enforcement to monitor the service of alcohol to underage drinkers. Working with undercover teenage volunteers, police monitor their attempts to buy alcohol with minor IDs, or sometimes with no identification at all. In New York, volunteers ranging in age from 16 to 18 were able to buy a drink from one out of every three servers they approached. Over 40 servers were arrested and charged during the three-day operation, each facing $1,000 fines and up to a year in jail.

A restaurant lost its liquor license for over 15 days for selling liquor after it was supposed to be closed for the evening. Sometime after 2:00 a.m., law enforcement officers on a routine night patrol noticed lights in the bar area of the establishment. Upon closer inspection, they saw several employees sitting at the bar with drinks in front of them. Local liquor laws required that all patrons be out of the establishment by 1:00 a.m. The establishment was cleared and the incident was reported to the liquor commission, which suspended the establishment's liquor license.

LAWS RESTRICTING ALCOHOL SERVICE

You must become familiar with the liquor laws that apply to your establishment. These may include:

1. **The legal age to drink.** In all 50 states, a person must be 21-years-old to purchase alcohol. In some states, it is legal for a parent or legal guardian to purchase alcohol and serve it to a minor child.

2. **The legal age to serve.** In general, you must be 21-years-old to serve alcohol. However, this law varies. Some states allow underage servers to:

   - Bring alcohol to the table but not to pour it

   - Take the order and payment for the drink, but not to serve the order

   - Serve alcohol if they have applied for permission from the liquor authority

HOW THIS RELATES TO ME...

In my state/municipality, you must be:

_18_ years-old to serve alcohol.

_18_ years-old to pour alcohol.

_18_ years-old to take a drink order.

3. **The legal age to enter the establishment.** In some areas, the law does not allow minors to enter a tavern or a restaurant bar area. Some establishments may require guests to be older than the age allowed by law to enter the bar.

HOW THIS RELATES TO ME...

At my establishment, minors are (allowed/not allowed) _____ inside.

At my establishment, a guest must be _____ years-old to enter.

At my establishment, minors are (allowed/not allowed) _____ in the bar area.

4. **Serving intoxicated guests.** It is illegal to serve a guest who is intoxicated or who shows signs of intoxication. (In chapter 2, you will learn how to identify visible signs of intoxication.)

5. **Serving a pregnant guest.** It is illegal to deny alcohol service to a woman because she is pregnant. This would be considered gender discrimination. Many states, however, require establishments to post signs warning about the effects of alcohol on a fetus.

It is illegal to serve an intoxicated guest.

HOW THIS RELATES TO ME...

In my state/municipality, warning signs about the effects of alcohol on a fetus (are/are not) ____Not____ required.

6. **Hours of service.** The legal hours for the sale and service of alcohol are listed on the establishment's liquor license. These must be strictly followed.

HOW THIS RELATES TO ME...

I cannot sell or serve alcohol before ___6am___ (a.m./p.m.) at my establishment.   Sundy 12

I must stop selling or serving alcohol at ___1am___ (a.m./p.m.) at my establishment.

7. **Happy hours and other drink promotions.** Some states, counties, and municipalities restrict or forbid "happy hours" and other drink promotions.

These laws may prohibit serving a guest:

- Two or more drinks at a time
- An unlimited number of drinks for a fixed price
- Reduced-priced drinks for a specified period of time
- Drinks containing additional alcohol without an increase in price
- Drinks as a prize for a game or a contest conducted at the establishment

HOW THIS RELATES TO ME...

Restrictions on drink promotions in my area include:

_____

_____

For information on your state's laws concerning the sale and service of alcohol, visit the ServSafe Alcohol Web site at **www.ServSafe.com/alcohol** and click on State Regulations.

SUMMARY

Here are some of the most important points from this chapter.

- **You can face criminal charges if you break liquor laws.** This might include serving alcohol to a minor or serving a guest to the point of intoxication. Breaking these laws could result in fines and even jail time.

- **You can be sued and forced to pay damages to an injured guest.** This is called civil liability.

- **Many states have dram shop laws.** These allow people injured by intoxicated guests to sue the establishment and employees who served the guests who injured them.

- **Every state has its own liquor laws.** You must become familiar with those that apply to your establishment.

- **Each state and many municipalities have a liquor authority that enforces alcohol laws.** These agencies are responsible for issuing and monitoring liquor licenses. They also issue citations for violations and hold hearings for violators.

- **Citations can be issued for violating liquor license laws.** This might include fines for both the server and the owner. A liquor license may also be suspended or revoked. In states that license servers to serve alcohol, the state may take away the server's license.

MULTIPLE-CHOICE STUDY QUESTIONS

1. **State or municipal liquor authorities can issue citations for**
   A. drunk driving.
   B. serving a pregnant woman.
   C. serving alcohol to a minor.
   D. fighting in the establishment.

2. **Which is a role of the liquor authority?**
   A. Issue liquor licenses
   B. Initiate law suits against drunk drivers
   C. Issue citations to minors for presenting fake IDs
   D. Initiate criminal charges against establishments who serve minors

3. **Which is a criminal violation related to the sale and service of alcohol?**
   A. Serving alcohol to a minor
   B. Failing to fill out an incident report
   C. Firing a server who overserved a guest
   D. Refusing to serve a guest who arrived intoxicated

4. **Which situation best describes dram shop liability?**
   A. A manager is fined for allowing the sale of drugs on the premises.
   B. A server is fined by the liquor authority for serving alcohol to a minor.
   C. A bartender is given jail time for serving a guest who appeared intoxicated.
   D. A person sues the bartender who served the intoxicated guest who injured him.

5. **Which is a possible consequence for violating the liquor code?**
   A. Jail time
   B. Probation
   C. Misdemeanor
   D. Liquor-license suspension

For answers, please turn to page 1-12.

ANSWERS

Page	Activity

1-2   Test Your Knowledge

1. True
2. False
3. False
4. True
5. True

1-5   List the Crime

1. Serving alcohol to a minor
2. Serving a guest who is or appears to be intoxicated
3. Possessing, selling, or allowing the sale of drugs on the premises

1-11   Multiple-Choice Study Questions

1. C
2. A
3. A
4. D
5. D

NOTES

2

Recognizing and Preventing Intoxication

After completing this chapter, you should be able to:

■ Identify alcohol's path through the body.

■ Identify the liver's role in breaking down alcohol in the body.

■ Identify factors that affect a guest's BAC.

■ Identify drinks that contain the same amount of alcohol.

■ Identify how to count drinks accurately.

■ Identify the physical and behavioral signs of intoxication.

■ Identify methods for preventing guests from becoming intoxicated.

TEST YOUR KNOWLEDGE

1. **True or False:** Drink for drink, a lean guest will have a higher BAC than a guest with a large amount of body fat. *(See page 2-5.)*

2. **True or False:** A 12-ounce beer contains less alcohol than 1½ ounces of 80-proof vodka. *(See page 2-8.)*

3. **True or False:** The liver can break down alcohol at the rate of two drinks per hour. *(See page 2-5.)*

4. **True or False:** Carbohydrates are the best type of food to serve with alcohol to help prevent intoxication. *(See page 2-19.)*

5. **True or False:** A guest who switches to larger or stronger drinks may be intoxicated. *(See page 2-14.)*

For answers, please turn to page 2-24.

CONCEPTS

- **Blood alcohol content (BAC):** Amount of alcohol that has been absorbed into the bloodstream. It is stated as a percentage.

- **Small intestine:** Organ from which most alcohol is absorbed into the bloodstream.

- **Liver:** Organ responsible for breaking down alcohol in the body. It does this at a rate of one drink per hour.

- **Tolerance:** Ability to deal with the effects of alcohol without showing signs.

- **Proof:** Measure of a liquor's strength. The percentage of alcohol in liquor can be determined by dividing its proof in half.

ALCOHOL AND THE BODY

To help prevent your guests from becoming intoxicated, you need to know:

- How alcohol moves through the body
- How alcohol is eliminated from the body
- Factors that affect alcohol's concentration in the bloodstream

Carbonated cocktails?

Alcohol's Path Through the Body

Alcohol moves through a person's body like food does. Unlike food, however, it does not need to be digested to reach the bloodstream.

Here's what happens when a person drinks alcohol.

1. Mouth
A small amount of alcohol is absorbed into the bloodstream from here.

2. Stomach
Some alcohol is absorbed into the bloodstream through the stomach wall.

3. Small intestine
Most of the alcohol is absorbed into the bloodstream from here.

4. Throughout the body
Once in the bloodstream, alcohol travels quickly throughout the body. It will reach the brain in minutes.

The amount of alcohol in a person's bloodstream is called blood alcohol content (BAC). It is stated as a percentage. A BAC of .10 means there is about one drop of alcohol for every 1,000 drops of blood in the bloodstream.

■ Driving with a BAC of .08 or higher is against the law in all 50 states.

■ A BAC of .30 or higher can lead to coma or death.

SOMETHING TO THINK ABOUT...

A 34-year-old intoxicated man was arrested by Rhode Island state police after hitting a road sign. His blood alcohol test revealed the highest reading ever obtained in the state—an unprecedented .491. Because of the dangerously high reading, he was immediately taken to a hospital. He was then restrained in a detoxification unit by the staff due to his aggressiveness.

APPLY YOUR KNOWLEDGE: *Believe It or Not?*

Place an X next to each activity that removes a large amount of alcohol from the body.

1. ___ Breathing   4. ___ Exercising

2. ___ Drinking coffee   5. ___ Urinating

3. ___ Taking a cold shower   6. ___ Passing of time

For answers, please turn to page 2-24.

The Liver's Role in Removing Alcohol from the Body

Only the liver can break down alcohol. It does this at a constant rate of about **one drink per hour**.

Factors That Affect a Guest's BAC

Several factors can affect the BAC of your guests. This includes:

- **Drinking rate and amount consumed.**

  - The liver can only remove alcohol from the body at the rate of one drink per hour. Drinking more than this will result in a buildup in the bloodstream. This will raise BAC.

  - Alcohol can affect guests long after they've stopped drinking. That's because alcohol will continue to enter their bloodstreams.

- **Drink strength.** The more alcohol a drink contains, the more that will end up in the bloodstream. This will raise BAC.

- **Body size.** A small person will have a higher BAC than a large person, all other factors being the same. That's because small people have less blood in their bodies to dilute alcohol.

- **Body fat.** A person with a large percentage of body fat will have a higher BAC than a lean person, all other factors being the same.

  - Body fat does not absorb alcohol. This forces it to remain in the bloodstream until broken down by the liver.

  - Alcohol can pass through muscle in a lean person and spread throughout the body.

- **Gender.** A woman will have a higher BAC than a man, all other factors being the same. That's because women:

  - Have a higher percentage of body fat.

  - Have a smaller amount of a stomach enzyme that helps break down alcohol.

  - Are typically smaller than men, and so have less blood in their bodies.

Drinking rate can affect BAC.

Drink strength can affect BAC.

■ **Age.** A senior citizen will have a higher BAC than a younger guest, all other factors being the same.

    ■ Body fat typically increases with age.

    ■ Enzyme action tends to slow as a person gets older.

■ **Emotional state.** An emotional guest will have a higher BAC than a guest who is calm, all other factors being the same.

    ■ When a person is stressed, angry, or afraid, the body diverts blood to the muscles and away from the stomach and small intestine.

    ■ This reduced blood flow slows the absorption of alcohol into the bloodstream.

■ **Medications.** Guests who drink alcohol while taking medications or using illegal drugs can intensify the effects of alcohol or experience dangerous interactions.

■ **Food.** A guest who has not eaten will have a higher BAC than a guest who has eaten, all other factors being the same.

    ■ Food keeps alcohol in the stomach for a longer period of time. This slows the rate at which it reaches the small intestine.

    ■ Take special care if you know a guest is dieting. Alcohol may pass more quickly from the stomach to the small intestine.

■ **Carbonation.** A guest who is drinking a carbonated drink will have a higher BAC than a guest whose drink is not carbonated, all other factors being the same.

    ■ Carbonation may speed the rate at which alcohol passes through the stomach. This causes a person to reach a higher BAC at a faster rate.

Keep in mind that some guests will have a combination of these factors. This will result in a higher risk of intoxication. These guests require even more attention on your part to prevent intoxication.

Medications can intensify the effects of alcohol.

Carbonation can affect BAC.

APPLY YOUR KNOWLEDGE: *Whose BAC Is Higher?*

Assuming that each pair of guests is drinking at the same rate, which guest will have a higher BAC? Explain your choice in the space provided.

Guest 1   Guest 2

1. _____

_____

_____

_____

_____

_____

Guest 1   Guest 2

2. _____

_____

_____

_____

_____

_____

Guest 1   Guest 2

3. _____

_____

_____

_____

_____

For answers, please turn to page 2-24.

ASSESSING A GUEST'S LEVEL OF INTOXICATION

To prevent overservice, you must be able to assess a guest's level of intoxication. There are two ways to do this:

1. Count the number of drinks you serve.

2. Observe behavior.

Using a combination of the two is the best approach for preventing guests from becoming intoxicated.

Counting Drinks

Counting drinks is a useful tool for determining if a guest is intoxicated. To count drinks, you need to know how much alcohol the drinks contain.

Proof is a measure of a liquor's strength. By dividing the proof by two, you can determine how much alcohol a liquor contains. For example:

- 100-proof whiskey = 50% alcohol (100 ÷ 2 = 50)
- 80-proof vodka = 40% alcohol (80 ÷ 2 = 40)

The following beverages serve as the standard measure when counting drinks. They contain about the same amount of alcohol and should be counted as one drink.

1 Drink =   or   or   or

5 ounces of wine (Domestic wine at 12% alcohol)

12 ounces of beer (American lager at 4–5% alcohol)

1½ ounces of 80–proof liquor

1 ounce of 100–proof liquor

Some beers, flavored malt beverages, and wines have a higher alcohol content, so you must count them differently than the standard beverages listed on the previous page. Also, adding a nonalcoholic beverage (mixer) to a drink does not alter its alcohol content.

The size of a drink and its contents will also affect the way it is counted.

■ **Size of the drink.** Some beverages contain more alcohol than the standard drinks shown on the previous page. To count these beverages correctly, you need to figure out the actual number of drinks in them. To do this, divide the liquor in the beverage by the standard amount of that liquor found in one drink.

For example, whiskey on the rocks containing three ounces of 80-proof whiskey would be counted as two drinks. Here's why:

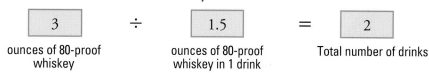

3	÷	1.5	=	2
ounces of 80-proof whiskey		ounces of 80-proof whiskey in 1 drink		Total number of drinks

Whiskey

Here's another example. You now know that a 12-ounce beer is counted as one drink, but how many drinks are there in a 24-ounce beer? The answer is two. Here's why:

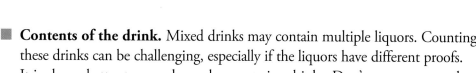

24	÷	12	=	2
ounces of beer		ounces of beer in 1 drink		Total number of drinks

■ **Contents of the drink.** Mixed drinks may contain multiple liquors. Counting these drinks can be challenging, especially if the liquors have different proofs. It is always better to round up when counting drinks. Don't worry too much about the math. Most establishments will make these calculations for you.

24-ounce beer

HOW THIS RELATES TO ME...

Does your establishment have formal drink recipes? Are they catalogued in a drink recipe file? Do they include a drink count?

_____

_____

_____

APPLY YOUR KNOWLEDGE: *Count the Drinks*

Calculate the number of drinks in each item and write the number in the space provided. Note: Round up or down if necessary.

1. ___5___ 60-ounce pitcher of beer
2. ___2___ 3 ounces of 80-proof vodka on the rocks
3. ___2___ 2 ounces of 100-proof whiskey
4. ___3___ 15-ounce carafe of wine
5. ___2___ 12-ounce beer and a shot of 100-proof whiskey

For answers, please turn to page 2-24.

Calculating BAC

You can estimate a guest's BAC by following these steps:

1. Count the number of drinks the guest was served.

2. Estimate his or her approximate weight.

3. Use the chart on the next page to calculate his or her BAC.

There is one chart for men and another for women. These charts are based on one hour of drinking. They also account for the liver breaking down alcohol at the rate of one drink per hour.

How many drinks can a guest safely consume? How much is too much? As you know, a BAC of .08 is the legal level of intoxication while driving in the United States. The values in the charts highlighted in red indicate a BAC of .08 or higher. You are not legally responsible for knowing your guest's BAC. But counting drinks and using these charts—along with watching for visible signs of intoxication (which you will learn about in the next section)—will help you make the best decisions while serving.

These charts should be used only as a reference. A guest's actual BAC may be higher or lower, because the chart cannot account for other factors that might affect the guest, such as:

■ Prior drinking

■ Physical condition and emotional state

■ Consumption of food or medication

Blood Alcohol Content (BAC) Estimation Charts — Slow the alcohol

MEN
(after one hour of drinking)

Body Weight

Number of Drinks	100	120	140	160	180	200	220	240
1	.022	.015	.011	.007	.005	.003	.001	.000
2	.059	.046	.038	.031	.026	.022	.018	.015
3	.097	.078	.064	.054	.046	.040	.035	.031
4	.134	.109	.091	.078	.067	.059	.052	.046
5	.172	.140	.118	.101	.088	.078	.069	.062
6	.209	.172	.145	.125	.109	.097	.086	.078
7	.247	.203	.172	.148	.130	.115	.103	.093
8	.284	.234	.198	.172	.151	.134	.120	.109

▇ Indicates a BAC of .08 or higher

Markham, M.R., Miller, W.R. & Arciniega, L. (1993) BACCuS 2.01: Computer software for quantifying alcohol consumption. Behavior Research Methods, Instruments, & Computers, 25, 420-421.

WOMEN
(after one hour of drinking)

Body Weight

Number of Drinks	100	120	140	160	180	200	220	240
1	.029	.022	.016	.012	.009	.006	.004	.003
2	.074	.059	.048	.040	.034	.029	.025	.022
3	.119	.097	.080	.068	.059	.052	.045	.040
4	.164	.134	.113	.096	.084	.074	.066	.059
5	.209	.172	.145	.125	.109	.097	.086	.078
6	.254	.209	.177	.153	.134	.119	.107	.097
7	.299	.247	.209	.181	.159	.142	.127	.115
8	.344	.284	.241	.209	.184	.164	.148	.134

▇ Indicates a BAC of .08 or higher

Markham, M.R., Miller, W.R. & Arciniega, L. (1993) BACCuS 2.01: Computer software for quantifying alcohol consumption. Behavior Research Methods, Instruments, & Computers, 25, 420-421.

Let's say that a 120-pound woman has consumed two drinks in an hour. Using the chart for women, her approximate BAC would be .059. On the other hand, it would take four drinks for a 200-pound man to reach the same BAC.

APPLY YOUR KNOWLEDGE: *What Are Their BACs?*

Estimate the BAC of each guest using the charts on page 2–11 and write it in the space provided.

1. _.10(_ 160-pound man who drank five 12-ounce beers in one hour

2. _.119_ 100-pound woman who drank three 5-ounce glasses of wine in one hour

3. _.059_ 180-pound woman who drank three mixed drinks, each containing 1½ ounces of 80-proof vodka in one hour

4. _.062_ 240-pound man who drank five shots (five ounces) of 100-proof bourbon in one hour

For answers, please turn to page 2-24.

Bar tabs can help bartenders and servers count drinks.

When to Count Drinks

You should start counting drinks when guests place their first order and continue counting until they leave the premises. There are many ways to do this.

■ In bar areas, a tab can be left in front of the guest so bartenders and servers can monitor it.

■ For dining guests, servers can keep a drink tally on the back of the guest check.

■ In some establishments, the guest check moves with the guest, which makes counting easier.

■ Servers can review their point-of-sale receipts.

In some situations, counting drinks can be difficult. If counting drinks won't work, then you must rely on observation to spot signs of intoxication.

HOW THIS RELATES TO ME...

What is your company policy regarding counting drinks? List some ways that you count drinks in your establishment.

_____

_____

Observing Guests for Signs of Intoxication

You can learn a lot about how alcohol is affecting your guests by watching them. Look for physical and behavioral changes. A change in behavior is more revealing than the actual behavior itself. There is a big difference between a normally loud guest and a guest who is quiet when he or she first arrives and then becomes loud after a few drinks.

Communication is also important. Taking the time to talk to your guests will help you determine the purpose of their visit as well as their level of intoxication. If guests are determined to become intoxicated, you want to know about it. Continue talking to each guest throughout his or her stay.

Physical and Behavioral Signs of Intoxication

When large amounts of alcohol reach the brain, it can no longer function normally. This causes physical and behavioral changes, including: relaxed inhibitions, impaired judgment, slowed reaction time, and impaired motor coordination.

■ **Relaxed inhibitions.** Inhibitions prevent people from saying or doing things that may be unacceptable to others. As people drink, their normal inhibitions will become relaxed. Guests with relaxed inhibitions may:

Guests with relaxed inhibitions may be overly friendly.

- Be overly friendly

- Be unfriendly, depressed, or quiet

- Use foul language

- Become loud

- Make rude comments

Guests with impaired judgment may become careless with money and buy drinks for strangers.

Guests with slowed reaction time will often become drowsy or fall asleep.

Guests with impaired motor coordination may spill drinks.

■ **Impaired judgment.** A guest's ability to make sensible decisions will be affected. Guests with impaired judgment may:

- Complain about the strength of a drink after drinking others of the same strength

- Begin drinking faster or switch to larger or stronger drinks

- Make irrational or argumentative statements

- Become careless with money (e.g., buying drinks for strangers)

■ **Slowed reaction time.** A guest's reaction time and responses will become slower. Guests with slowed reaction time may:

- Talk or move slowly

- Be unable to concentrate, lose their train of thought, or become forgetful

- Become drowsy

- Become glassy eyed, lose eye contact, or become unable to focus

■ **Impaired motor coordination.** A guest's motor skills will be affected. Guests with impaired motor coordination may:

- Stagger, stumble, fall down, bump objects, or sway when sitting or standing

- Be unable to pick up objects or may drop them

- Spill drinks or miss their mouths when drinking

- Slur their speech

- Having difficulty lighting a cigarette

Tolerance to Alcohol

People can build up a tolerance to alcohol. Tolerance is the ability to handle the effects of alcohol without showing the usual signs. An experienced drinker can often consume a lot of alcohol without showing any signs. These people have learned to hide them—even after becoming intoxicated. This makes it difficult for you to assess this type of guest by observation alone. Remember: tolerance does not affect a guest's BAC, just his or her ability to hide the effects of alcohol.

Regulars

Most establishments have guests who are regular patrons. You can become used to their drinking habits and ability to handle liquor. But these people may be leaving your establishment with a dangerously high BAC. In fact, the majority of alcohol-related incidents involve regular patrons. Always count drinks, because it may be difficult to spot signs of intoxication.

Inexperienced Drinkers

Another type of guest that should be watched closely is the inexperienced drinker. They often show signs of intoxication after drinking only a small amount of alcohol. Their bodies are not used to alcohol and are sensitive to smaller amounts.

Watch inexperienced drinkers closely.

SOMETHING TO THINK ABOUT...

Steve was a regular patron at Half Time Bar and Grill, which he visited at least three times a week. Everyone knew Steve and liked him. Kelly—on her first day on the job—served him a small salad and five beers in the course of an hour. She noticed that Steve was more relaxed but otherwise seemed fine. Kelly was amazed at Steve's tolerance.

Later, she said to Mary, a more experienced server, "Man, he can sure drink a lot." Mary replied, "Yeah, he's been coming here for years. He's fine. He must have a liver of steel." While Kelly was concerned about how much Steve had been drinking, she overlooked it after talking to Mary.

After three hours and eleven beers, Steve left the restaurant. The next morning, the manager on duty received a call from the local police. The previous evening, Steve was in a car accident and had killed the mother of two children and injured himself. He had a BAC of .21 at the time of the accident.

The Importance of Observation and Communication

Monitor guests from the moment they arrive until they are ready to leave. Tell management and the appropriate coworkers if a guest shows signs of intoxication. If guests move to another location in the establishment, pass along any information about the amount of alcohol they have consumed. To be successful when evaluating guests, you will need input from coworkers who have come in contact with them. This includes:

- Valets

- Waitstaff

- Bus staff

- Bartenders

- Security, hosts and hostesses, and greeters

- Coat check and restroom attendants

Valets

Valets often are the first people to make contact with guests. If you are a valet, you should watch for intoxicated guests. Then, alert your manager before they enter the establishment and attempt to be served.

As you observe guests, ask yourself the following questions:

- Is their driving erratic?

- Are they having difficulty parking between the lines in the parking space?

- Are they having difficulty getting out of the car or walking?

- Are they having difficulty talking?

- Do you smell alcohol?

If you can answer *Yes* to any one of these questions, there may be cause for concern and you should notify your manager. Handling this type of situation will be addressed in chapter 4.

Valets can spot signs of intoxication by watching guests get out of their car.

Security, Hosts and Hostesses, and Greeters

If you work in any of the following positions, you are often the first person to make contact with guests once they have stepped inside the establishment:

■ Security staff

■ Hosts and hostesses

■ Greeters

Use your greeting as an opportunity to talk to the guests and watch for the following:

■ Are they speaking rationally?

■ Is their speech slurred?

■ Are they able to make eye contact and focus while talking to you?

■ Can they walk without staggering, stumbling, or bumping into objects?

Hosts and hostesses should talk to guests to look for signs of intoxication.

Bus Staff

Bus staff are in a unique position to observe guest behavior. If you are busing tables, use the opportunity to listen to how guests speak and watch for the following:

■ Are they getting louder as time passes?

■ Are they becoming overly friendly, or are they starting to use foul language or becoming rude?

■ Have they started spilling drinks or food on the table?

■ Are they having difficulty talking?

■ Are they beginning to look tired or sleepy?

If you notice any of these behaviors, talk to your manager.

Bus staff can spot signs of intoxication by observing and listening to guests.

HOW THIS RELATES TO ME...

How do you communicate information about intoxicated guests in your establishment?

_____

_____

APPLY YOUR KNOWLEDGE: _Rate the Guest_

This activity requires Video/DVD 5: _Evaluating Real-World Scenarios._
After watching each scenario from section 1 of this video/DVD, use the rating scale below to rate whether or not the guest(s) are intoxicated by placing the appropriate number in the space provided.

Rating scale
1 = Guest is not intoxicated (is sober).
2 = Guest is intoxicated.

Video Segment	Description	Rating
1	Valet interacting with a guest leaving the establishment	2 ✓
2	Two female guests eating in a fine-dining restaurant	2 ✓
3	Senior citizen sitting at a table	2̶ 1
4	Guest talking to a female server at the end of the bar	2 ✓
5	Two male guests watching a football game at a bar	1 ✓
6	Female guest talking with a bartender at the bar	2 ✓
7	Male and female guests drinking in a nightclub	2 ✓
8	Male guest entering an establishment	1 (2) ✓
9	Construction worker drinking at the bar	1 ✓
10	Regular interacting with a bartender at the bar	2 ✓

 # wiring

**For answers, please turn to page 2-24.**

PREVENTING GUESTS FROM BECOMING INTOXICATED

As a seller or server of alcohol, you must do everything possible to ensure that guests do not become intoxicated. This can sometimes be a difficult task, but you can do some simple things. These practices will help guests drink responsibly. They are also a part of good service.

- **Offer food.** This is one of the most important things you can do to help prevent intoxication. Food helps keep alcohol in the stomach. This slows the rate at which it reaches the small intestine.

  - **Offer food high in fat and/or protein (e.g., pizza, chicken wings, cheese, deep-fried items).** These items are not easily digested. This slows the movement of alcohol into the small intestine.

  - **Avoid food that is high in sugar or carbohydrates (e.g., bread).** These items are easily digested. They are less effective in slowing the movement of alcohol into the small intestine.

  - **Avoid food items that are salty (e.g., peanuts, pretzels, chips).** These items can make a guest thirsty and cause them to drink more alcohol.

- **Offer water.** Drinking alcohol causes dehydration, making guests thirsty. This can cause them to drink more than they ordinarily would. You can help by offering water with drinks and refilling water glasses often.

- **Avoid overpouring when mixing drinks.** Overpouring makes it difficult for:

  - Staff to count the actual number of drinks consumed by guests

  - Guests to keep track of, and regulate, their own drinking

  - Bartenders to create consistent drinks

    For example, let's say that the recipe for a gin and tonic calls for 1½ ounces of 80-proof gin. If you mix three gin and tonics for a guest, but you overpour the gin in each drink by a half ounce, you have actually served the guest four drinks instead of three.

- **Avoid serving the guest more than one drink at a time.** This will help pace the guest's consumption.

Food high in fat is one of the best types of food to serve with alcohol.

Offer water with drinks.

APPLY YOUR KNOWLEDGE: *Which Food Is Best?*

Place an X next to the food items that are best for preventing intoxication.

1. ___ Bread
2. ___ Pizza
3. ___ Potato chips
4. ___ Cheese sticks
5. ___ Chili
6. ___ Onion rings
7. ___ Pretzels
8. ___ Peanuts
9. ___ Fried calamari
10. ___ Chicken wings

For answers, please turn to page 2-26.

HOW THIS RELATES TO ME...

List the types of appetizers served in your establishment that can help prevent intoxication.

SUMMARY

Here are some of the most important points from this chapter.

- **Only the liver can break down alcohol.** It does this at a constant rate of about one drink per hour. Consuming more than this will cause a buildup of alcohol in the bloodstream.

- **Several factors affect BAC.** These include the rate of consumption, drink strength, and amount consumed. Body type, gender, age, and the guest's emotional state are also factors, as are the amount of food consumed and whether or not a drink is carbonated.

- **Counting drinks and observing guests for physical and behavioral changes are the two ways to assess a guest's level of intoxication.** A combination of these two approaches is best for preventing intoxication.

■ **To count drinks accurately, you need to know how much alcohol they contain.** These beverages contain approximately the same amount of alcohol and should be counted as one drink: a 12-ounce beer, a 5-ounce glass of wine, 1½ ounces of 80-proof liquor, and 1 ounce of 100-proof liquor. While these beverages are the standard measures when counting drinks, some will be counted differently.

■ **You can estimate a guest's BAC by using a BAC estimation chart.** If you can identify a guest's approximate weight and have counted the number of drinks he or she has consumed, you can get a rough estimate of the person's BAC using an estimation chart. These charts should be used only as a general reference.

■ **You can learn a lot about a guest's level of intoxication by watching for physical and behavioral changes.** A change in behavior is more significant than the actual behavior itself.

■ **When large amounts of alcohol reach the brain, physical and behavioral changes occur.** These include relaxed inhibitions, impaired judgment, slowed reaction time, and impaired motor coordination.

■ **Guests with relaxed inhibitions may show these signs:** be overly friendly; be unfriendly, depressed, or quiet; use foul language; become loud; or make rude comments.

■ **Guests with impaired judgment may show these signs:** complain about drink strength after drinking others of the same strength; begin drinking faster or switch to larger or stronger drinks; make irrational or argumentative statements; or become careless with money.

■ **Guests with slowed reaction time may show these signs:** talk or move slowly; be unable to concentrate, lose their train of thought or become forgetful; become drowsy; become glassy-eyed; lose eye contact; or become unable to focus.

■ **Guests with impaired motor coordination may show these signs:** stagger, stumble, fall down, or bump into objects; be unable to pick up objects or may drop them; spill drinks or miss their mouths when drinking; sway when sitting or standing; slur their speech; or have difficulty lighting a cigarette.

■ **An experienced drinker can often consume a large quantity of alcohol without showing its effects.** This is called tolerance. You must be careful when dealing with regular drinkers at your establishment who may have a high tolerance. Always count drinks.

■ **Offering food is one of the most important things you can do to prevent guests from becoming intoxicated.** Food keeps alcohol in the stomach for a longer period of time, slowing the rate at which it reaches the small intestine. The best food items are fatty and high in protein. These types of food are digested more slowly.

MULTIPLE-CHOICE STUDY QUESTIONS

1. Most of the alcohol a person drinks is absorbed into the bloodstream from the

   A. lungs.

   B. mouth.

   C. small intestine.

   D. liver.

2. The liver can break down alcohol at the rate of ___ drink(s) per hour.

   A. 1

   B. 2

   C. 3

   D. 4

3. A guest has consumed three 12-ounce beers in an hour. How many drinks have built up in the guest's bloodstream?

   A. 0

   B. 1

   C. 2

   D. 3

4. Assuming that the people involved weigh the same and have consumed the same number of drinks, which is true?

   A. A man will have a higher BAC than a woman.

   B. A lean man will have a higher BAC than a man with a large amount of body fat.

   C. A woman who has eaten will have a higher BAC than a woman who has not.

   D. A man drinking gin and tonic will have a higher BAC than a man drinking vodka and cranberry juice.

5. Which can be counted as one drink?

   A. 20-ounce beer

   B. 6-ounce glass of wine

   C. 2 ounces of 80-proof liquor

   D. 1 ounce of 100-proof liquor

Continued on next page…

MULTIPLE-CHOICE STUDY QUESTIONS
continued

6. A vodka on the rocks containing 3 ounces of 80-proof vodka should be counted as ___ drink(s).

   A. 1   C. 3

   B. 2   D. 4

7. Which behavior is a sign that a guest is experiencing relaxed inhibitions?

   A. Becoming loud

   B. Slurring speech

   C. Having difficulty making eye contact

   D. Drinking faster and switching to stronger drinks

8. Which behavior is a sign that a guest is experiencing impaired motor coordination?

   A. Becoming drowsy

   B. Swaying

   C. Making rude comments

   D. Having trouble concentrating

9. What is the best type of food to help prevent intoxication?

   A. Salty food

   B. Carbohydrates

   C. Sugars

   D. Fatty food

10. Which action can help prevent a guest from becoming intoxicated?

   A. Serving one drink at a time

   B. Offering bread or other carbohydrates

   C. Overpouring drinks

   D. Offering a guest approaching intoxication a beer instead of a martini

For answers, please turn to page 2-26.

ANSWERS

Page	Activity

2-2 **Test Your Knowledge**

1. False 2. False 3. False 4. False 5. True

2-4 **Believe It or Not?**

6

2-7 **Whose BAC Is Higher?**

1. Guest 2 will probably have a higher BAC. Guest 2 is smaller than Guest 1, which means that she has less blood in her body to dilute the alcohol that she has consumed. Also, Guest 2 is drinking champagne—a carbonated beverage. Carbonation may cause the alcohol to pass into the bloodstream more quickly.

2. Guest 2 will probably have a higher BAC. Although they are similar in size, the woman would have a higher percentage of body fat and a smaller amount of a stomach enzyme that helps to break down alcohol. Therefore, she would have a higher BAC. Also, she is drinking a martini. Compared to Guest 1's glass of wine, the martini contains more alcohol, so more of it will end up in her bloodstream.

3. Guest 1 will probably have a higher BAC. A guest's BAC depends upon the quantity of alcohol entering the bloodstream. Guest 1 is drinking a larger amount of beer (24 ounces) and is not eating. Since he is not eating, the alcohol he is drinking may pass more quickly from his stomach to his small intestine. On the other hand, Guest 2 is drinking a smaller beer (12 ounces) and is also eating. Food keeps alcohol in the stomach for a longer period of time, slowing the rate at which it reaches the small intestine.

2-10 **Count the Drinks**

1. 5 2. 2 3. 2 4. 3 5. 2

2-12 **What Are Their BACs?**

1. This man has had five drinks, since a 12-ounce beer is considered one drink. His approximate BAC would be .101.

2. This woman has had three drinks, since a five-ounce glass of wine is considered one drink. Her approximate BAC is .119.

3. This woman has had three drinks, since 1½ ounces of 80-proof liquor is considered one drink. Her approximate BAC is .059.

4. This man actually had five drinks, since each 100-proof shot is considered one drink. His approximate BAC would be .062.

2-18 **Rate the Guest**

1. Rating: 2—Intoxicated.

   Indicators of intoxication:

   ■ The guest was staggering and swaying.
   ■ The guest spilled money from his pocket on the ground and had difficulty picking it up.
   ■ The guest was loud.
   ■ The guest had impaired speech.

Continued on next page...

ANSWERS continued

!

Page   Activity

2. Rating: 2—Intoxicated.

Indicators of intoxication:

- The guest repeatedly spilled wine.
- The guests were inappropriately loud.
- The guest's speech was impaired (had difficulty choosing her words).

3. Rating: 1—Sober.

Indicators of sobriety:

- At this point, the guest was not showing any signs of intoxication. The fact that he had taken medication, however, should have alerted the server that he is at risk for intoxication.
- The fact that the guest ordered a double should also be of concern to the server.

4. Rating: 2—Intoxicated.

Indicators of intoxication:

- The guest was overly friendly.
- The guest made rude comments.
- The guest's speech was impaired.

5. Rating: 1—Sober.

Indicators of sobriety:

- The guests were speaking clearly (no sign of slurring).
- The guests were eating fatty food, which slows the absorption of alcohol.
- The guests used good judgment and had a single beer each rather than ordering another pitcher.

6. Rating: 2—Intoxicated.

Indicators of intoxication:

- The guest complained about the strength of her drinks.
- The guest became argumentative.

7. Rating: 2—Intoxicated.

Indicators of intoxication:

- The man and the woman became too intimate for people who didn't know each other.

8. Rating: 2—Intoxicated.

Indicators of intoxication:

- The guest used profanity.
- The guest bumped into obstacles in his path.
- The guest was loud and unfriendly.

9. Rating: 1—Sober.

Indicators of sobriety:

- While the guest ordered four drinks (three shots of 100-proof bourbon and a 12-ounce beer), he only consumed about three-and-a-half drinks, since his beer was still half full. Since the guest was clearly over 200 pounds, muscular, and had most likely consumed food, he was not intoxicated.
- While the guest's rate of consumption could have caused concern, it was not an issue at the time.

Continued on next page...

ANSWERS *continued*

10. Rating: 2—Intoxicated.

Indicators of intoxication:

■ While the guest was not exhibiting any physical or behavioral signs of intoxication, he probably was intoxicated based on his size and drink count. He consumed four martinis, which, depending on the recipe, may be counted as six to eight drinks.

■ The guest had a high tolerance to alcohol.

2-20   Which Food Is Best?

1. No. Bread is a carbohydrate, which is easily digested.

2. Yes. The cheese on pizza makes it a fatty food, which is digested more slowly.

3. No. While potato chips are fried, they are carbohydrates and are salty, making them a poor choice.

4. Yes. Cheese is a fatty food. It is also deep-fried, making it a good choice.

5. Yes. The meat in the chili is a protein, which is digested more slowly.

6. Yes. The deep-fried onion rings are fatty and are therefore digested more slowly.

7. No. Pretzels are carbohydrates, which are digested quickly. They are also salty, which can cause thirst and increase the consumption of alcohol.

8. No. The peanuts are not really a good choice. They are salty, which can cause thirst and increase the consumption of alcohol.

9. Yes. Deep-fried calamari contains protein and it is a fatty food, which is digested more slowly.

10. Yes. The chicken is a protein, which takes time to digest. The chicken also has been deep-fried, making it a good choice.

2-22   Multiple-Choice Study Questions

1. C		6. B	
2. A		7. A	
3. C		8. B	
4. D		9. D	
5. D		10. A	

NOTES

_____

_____

_____

_____

_____

_____

_____

_____

_____

_____

_____

_____

_____

_____

_____

_____

_____

_____

3

Checking Identification

After completing this chapter, you should be able to:

- Identify acceptable forms of identification.
- Identify the characteristics of a valid ID.
- Identify valid IDs issued to minors.
- Verify that an ID is genuine.
- Verify that an ID belongs to the guest who has presented it.
- Identify when to check IDs.
- Identify the proper procedure for checking IDs.
- Use ID readers properly.
- Identify the proper way to deal with a fake ID.

TEST YOUR KNOWLEDGE

1. **True or False:** A birth certificate is an acceptable form of ID. *(See page 3-5.)*

2. **True or False:** An ID must have a state seal to be valid. *(See page 3-5.)*

3. **True or False:** An ID with split lamination is not valid. *(See page 3-5.)*

4. **True or False:** IDs containing the words "Official," "Authentic," or "Secure" are not genuine. *(See page 3-9.)*

5. **True or False:** A guest who appears nervous while you are reviewing his or her ID may be a minor. *(See page 3-14.)*

For answers, please turn to page 3-20.

CONCEPTS

■ **Hologram:** Three-dimensional text and images placed on IDs to prevent tampering. The image appears to change when the ID is tilted.

■ **Lamination:** Plastic film enclosing many state-issued IDs.

■ **Ghost photo image:** Copy of the person's photo added to an ID as a security feature. It is usually smaller and fainter than the original photo.

■ **ID checking guide:** Reference tool used to validate IDs. It includes samples and descriptions of current state drivers' licenses. It also includes detailed descriptions of minor and state ID cards.

■ **ID reader:** Device used to validate IDs. It does this by reading information enclosed in an ID's bar code or magnetic stripe.

APPLY YOUR KNOWLEDGE: *Spot the Minor*

Which of these people is a minor?

For answers, please turn to page 3-20.

INTRODUCTION

While all of the women in the photos look at least 21 years of age, all of them are minors. The woman in photo #1 is only 17-years-old! Many minors today look much older than they actually are. For this reason, it's dangerous to make a decision about service on a guess or a hunch about a guest's age.

As a seller or server of alcohol, you are responsible for ensuring that your guests are of legal age to drink. If you have any doubt about a guest's age, you must take the appropriate steps to verify it. You should know that:

■ You can be held criminally liable for serving a minor.

■ You have the legal right to refuse service if you suspect a guest is underage.

ACCEPTABLE FORMS OF IDENTIFICATION

Your state, city, or town determines the types of ID that can be used to confirm a guest's age. In most states, the following forms of ID are acceptable:

Driver's license

State ID card

Passport

Military ID

Military IDs and passports are acceptable forms of ID. But they may be uncommon in some areas. For this reason, you should always use an ID checking guide to validate them. An immigration card is also an acceptable form of ID in some areas. Ask your manager if you can accept them.

IDs that are valid in one state may not be valid in another. For example, some areas do not acknowledge out-of-state drivers' licenses or state ID cards as acceptable forms of ID. Check with your manager.

In most states, the following forms of ID are **not** acceptable:

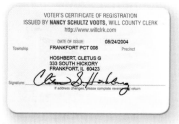

Birth certificate   **School ID**   **Voter's registration card**

VERIFYING IDENTIFICATION

When checking an ID, you must verify that it:

■ Is valid.   ■ Is genuine.

■ Has not been issued to a minor.   ■ Belongs to the guest.

Each of these topics will be discussed in detail.

Determining if an ID is Valid

An ID must be valid before you can accept it. A valid ID has the following features:

It contains the owner's birth date.

■ The birth date can be used to calculate the age of the guest.

It is current.

■ An expired license is never valid.

■ Minors often use the expired license of a family member or a friend who has been issued a new one.

It contains the owner's signature.

■ The signature can be used to verify that the person who presented it is the owner.

It contains the owner's photo.

■ The photo is used to verify that the person who presented the ID is the owner.

It is intact.

■ Several states use IDs that are laminated, or enclosed in plastic.

■ Lamination must be the proper thickness and must not be split or contain bubbles or creases.

■ In most states, a damaged ID is not valid and must be replaced.

APPLY YOUR KNOWLEDGE: *Valid or Invalid?*

Circle the ID(s) that are not valid.

1

2

3

For answers, please turn to page 3-20.

APPLY YOUR KNOWLEDGE: *List the Features*

List the five features of a valid ID.

1. _____   4. _____

2. _____   5. _____

3. _____

For answers, please turn to page 3-20.

Determining if an ID Has Been Issued to a Minor

All states add special features on a minor's ID to make an underage guest easy to spot. This includes adding designated colors and specific text. It also includes changing the layout of the ID.

■ **Colors**

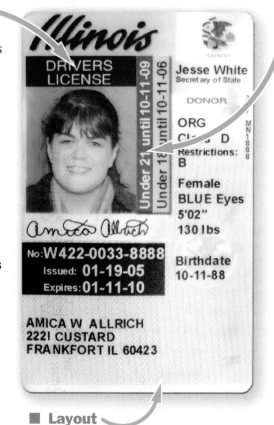

■ **Text**

- **Title bars.** Many states use specific colors in title bars, headers, and bands used to highlight text on the ID.

- **Text.** Some states display the minor's birth date, name and address, and other text in a special color.

- **Outlines and borders around photos.** Several states use red frames, outlines, or borders around photos on minor IDs.

- Most states include the words, "UNDER 21 UNTIL (date)" on the ID.

■ **Layout**

- **Format of the ID.** The IDs issued to minors in most states are in a vertical format rather than the horizontal format used for those 21 years of age or older.

- **Photo placement.** In some states, a minor's photo is placed on the opposite side of where it is placed for someone 21 years or older.

HOW THIS RELATES TO ME...

List the security features used on minor IDs in your state.

_____

_____

Using the Birth Date to Verify a Guest's Age

Almost all state IDs include the date that the minor will turn 21-years-old. This eliminates the need to calculate the guest's age from his or her birth date.

Your establishment may also post signs or calendars stating that a guest must have been born on or before a certain date to be served alcohol in your establishment. These can be excellent aids to help you determine if a guest is old enough to drink. They are typically available through your liquor distributor. Talk to your manager.

APPLY YOUR KNOWLEDGE: *To Serve or Not to Serve?*

It is December 15, 2009. Place an X next to each guest who is old enough to be served alcohol.

_____ 1. Guest born on September 19, 1987

_____ 2. Guest born on March 13, 1988

_____ 3. Guest born on December 25, 1988

_____ 4. Guest born on October 15, 1989

_____ 5. Guest born on December 15, 1990

For answers, please turn to page 3-20.

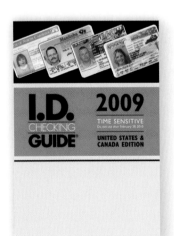

Verifying That the ID is Genuine

In recent years, states have developed IDs that are difficult to alter or falsify. But people have also become better at creating genuine-looking ones. The key to spotting fake IDs is to know what the valid IDs in your state and in neighboring states look like.

- **Talk to your manager about the valid IDs issued by your state.**

- **Use an ID checking guide.** These guides provide full-size samples and descriptions of current state drivers' licenses. They also include detailed descriptions of minor and state ID cards.

Characteristics of Genuine IDs

To determine if an ID is genuine, look for the following characteristics:

■ **Special text or images.** States place special text and images on IDs to make them hard to alter. When checking an ID with one of these features, make sure the text or image is appropriate, has been placed in the correct location, and is not distorted.

These features include:

■ **Optical variable devices (OVD).** Text and images that change color when the ID is tilted.

■ **UV features.** Text and images that can be seen only under ultraviolet (UV) light.

■ **Holograms.** Three-dimensional text and images that appear to change when the ID is tilted.

■ **Microprinting.** Specific text that is too small to be seen without a special device.

■ **Ghost photos.** Small, faint copies of the person's original photo.

The text on the ID should also have the correct font and spacing. Counterfeiters often place improper text or icons on IDs to avoid criminal liability.

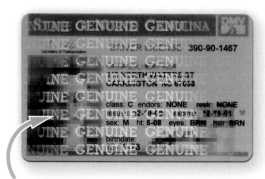

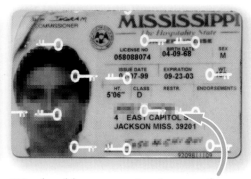

IDs should *not* contain the following words:

■ Genuine   ■ Authentic

■ Official   ■ Souvenir

■ Valid   ■ Novelty

■ Secure

IDs should *not* contain pictures of:

■ Locks

■ Keys

■ **License numbers.** All states include a license number on the ID. This may consist of:

○ Series of random numbers.

○ Series of letters and numbers. These may be random. They may also be coded to personal information (last name, birth date, etc.).

○ Numbers coded to the holder's personal information.

When checking IDs, make sure that the license number contains the appropriate letter(s) and/or number of digits. You should also make sure they are spaced correctly. If the number is coded to personal information, make sure it is coded correctly.

■ **Proper photos.**

○ A blurry photo may indicate the ID has been altered.

○ Raised edges around the photo may indicate the photo has been replaced.

■ **Lamination.** Several states place a laminate over their IDs.

○ Make sure there are no cuts or tears in the lamination.

○ Make sure the ID is actually supposed to be laminated. Some counterfeiters place a laminate over the ID to hide alterations.

■ **Appropriate information on the back.** All state IDs have information on their backs. Most states also place bar codes and/or magnetic stripes there.

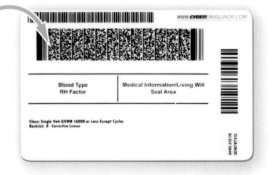

○ The code and/or stripe contains specific information about the person.

○ They can be accessed using an ID reader (see page 3-16).

You should be aware that the backs of fake IDs are sometimes blank. They may also contain a statement that identifies them as fake, such as, "For Entertainment Purposes Only." Always check the back of an ID to make sure it's genuine.

APPLY YOUR KNOWLEDGE:
Check It Out!

Using this page from the *I.D. Checking Guide,* identify the features on the ID that should be verified to ensure the ID is genuine.

_____

_____

_____

_____

_____

_____

_____

_____

_____

_____

_____

_____

KENTUCKY

Description: Licenses are digitized with 1D and 2D bar codes on back. Licenses do not show out-of-state address. For CDL, green heading, map enclosing "CDL," and "COMMERCIAL DRIVER'S LICENSE."

Minor's license: Vertical format with red "UNDER AGE 18 until (date)" and "UNDER AGE 21 until (date)" at photo right.

Validation: "THE BLUEGRASS STATE" visible under UV light; repeating security feature of stylized "K" within a box and "KEN-TUCKY TRANSPORTATION CABINET"; microprinting.

Number: 9 characters beginning with alpha (generally first initial of last name), followed by 2-digit year of original issuance, ending with 6 randomly assigned digits, hyphenated in groups of 3.

Term: Age 21 and over: 4 years, expiring on last day of birth month or 31 days after birthday. Under 21: Up to 5 years, expiring up to 90 days after 21st birthday. Photo update required with each issuance.

For answers, please turn to page 3-20.

HOW THIS RELATES TO ME...

List the security features used on IDs issued by your state.

_____

_____

_____

SOMETHING TO THINK ABOUT...

A university freshman in South Carolina died from alcohol poisoning at an off-campus fraternity party. He had a blood alcohol content of 0.38. Three fraternity members were charged in the death. One of them had used a fake ID to purchase beer for the party from a grocery store. He was charged with using a fake ID, underage possession of beer, and transfer of beer to a person under 21. The trio faced fines and up to one month in jail.

Verifying That the ID Belongs to the Guest

A common practice used by minors is to present the valid ID of a family member or friend. They might also use an expired license from a person who has been issued a new one.

To verify that the ID belongs to a guest:

■ **Compare the guest to the photo on the ID.** Certain features on a person usually do not change over time. You should look at these features when making the comparison:

- Chin
- Nose
- Eyes
- Hairline
- Shape of the face

■ **Compare the guest to the physical characteristics listed on the ID.**

Make sure the following features match:

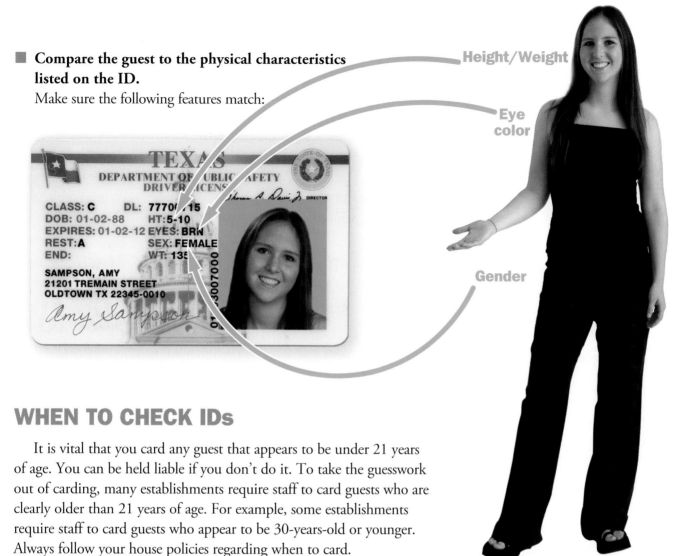

WHEN TO CHECK IDs

It is vital that you card any guest that appears to be under 21 years of age. You can be held liable if you don't do it. To take the guesswork out of carding, many establishments require staff to card guests who are clearly older than 21 years of age. For example, some establishments require staff to card guests who appear to be 30-years-old or younger. Always follow your house policies regarding when to card.

HOW THIS RELATES TO ME...

When should IDs be checked in your establishment?

_____

_____

_____

_____

THE PROPER PROCEDURE FOR CHECKING IDs

IDs must be checked according to the procedure below. Any time guests leave the establishment and then return, you should recheck their IDs. *You have the legal right to refuse service if you suspect the guest is a minor.*

1. **Greet the guest.** The greeting can tell you if the guest is nervous. This may indicate he or she is a minor.

2. **Politely ask the guest for ID.** You need to hold the ID to verify it. Ask the guest to remove the ID from his or her wallet. Be sure you look at both sides of the ID.

3. **Verify the ID.** Make sure it:

   ☐ Is valid.

   ☐ Has not been issued to a minor.

   ☐ Is genuine.

   ☐ Belongs to the guest.

   ID checking guides, ID readers, UV lights, and magnifying devices may make it easier to verify IDs.

4. **Seek further verification if necessary.** You can take several steps if you're still not sure about the ID:

   ☐ Ask the guest for a second valid ID.

   ☐ Compare the guest's signature to the ID signature.

   ☐ Ask the guest questions:

      ☐ What is your address?

      ☐ How tall are you?

      ☐ What is your middle name?

Refusing Service To A Minor

When you refuse service to a minor, be firm, but always express regret. Do not sound authoritative or judgmental. You should also avoid embarrassing the person. You might say something like:

- *"I'm sorry, but it's illegal to serve a minor."*
- *"I'm sorry, but I can't serve you without a valid ID."*
- *"I'm sorry, but our company policy will not allow me to serve you."*

Whenever you refuse service to a minor, notify your manager.

APPLY YOUR KNOWLEDGE: *Spot the Fake*

Circle the ID(s) that are fake.

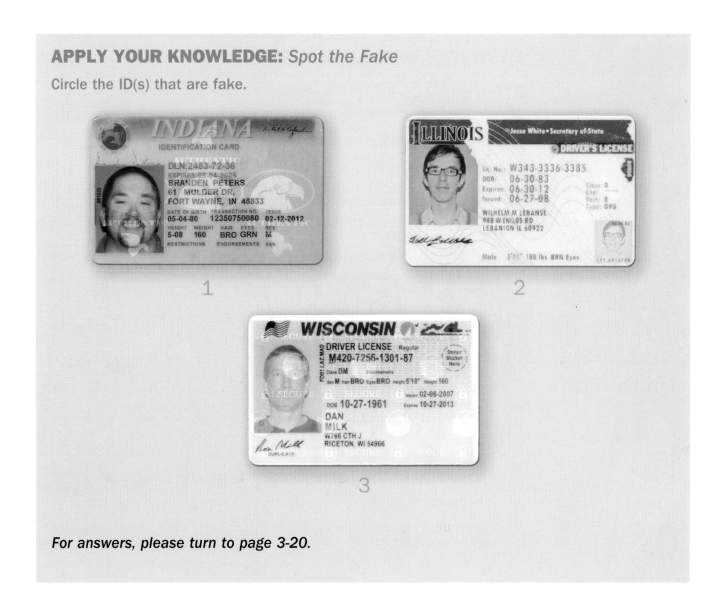

1

2

3

For answers, please turn to page 3-20.

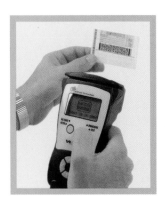

Always compare the readout on the ID reader with the information on the ID

USING ID READERS

Some establishments use ID readers to "read" the information stored in the bar codes and magnetic stripes on IDs. These tools can help verify the age of a guest. But you should still follow the other procedures for verifying IDs discussed in this chapter. When using ID readers:

■ **Compare the readout with the information displayed on the actual ID.** People sometimes import bar codes from valid ID cards. This will provide a false reading.

■ **Check magnetic stripes for signs of tampering.** People sometimes scratch the stripe to prevent the ID reader from reading it.

DEALING WITH A FAKE ID

If you spot a fake ID, you can take several steps. These may include:

■ Refusing service

■ Refusing entry to your establishment

■ Confiscating the ID

Always follow your company policy and the law in your area.

SOMETHING TO THINK ABOUT...

Penalties for an establishment selling alcohol to a minor vary by state. Here are some first-offense examples.

■ **Vermont:** Fine of $500 to $2,000 and up to two years in jail, or both

■ **Louisiana:** $400 fine

■ **Michigan:** $1,000 fine and possible license suspension or revocation

■ **Utah:** Fine of $500 to $3,000 and license suspension of up to 30 days

■ **Florida:** $1,000 fine and seven days license suspension

APPLY YOUR KNOWLEDGE: *Rate the Response*

This activity requires the Video/DVD 5: *Evaluating Real-World Scenarios.* After watching each scenario from section 2 of this video/DVD, rate how well the employee handled the situation by placing the appropriate number in the space provided.

Rating scale
1 = Employee handled the situation effectively.
2 = Employee handled the situation ineffectively.

Video Segment	Description	Rating
1	Parents attempting to serve an underage child in a fine-dining restaurant	
2	Group of friends attempting to enter a nightclub	
3	Flirtatious guest attempting to be served at the bar	
4	Guests attempting to enter a nightclub	
5	Guest attempting to be served at a sports bar	

For answers, please turn to page 3-21.

SUMMARY

Here are some of the most important points from this chapter.

- **You are responsible for ensuring that your guests are of legal age to drink.** If you serve an underage guest, you can be held criminally liable. Remember: you have the right to refuse service if you suspect the guest is underage. Always follow your company policies.

- **In most states, only certain forms of ID are acceptable.** This includes a driver's license, state ID card, passport, and military ID.

- **A valid ID has specific features.** It must be intact and current. It must also contain the owner's photograph, signature, and birth date.

- **States place certain features on minor IDs to make an underage guest easy to identify.** This includes the use of designated colors, text, and specific layout features. Many states also include the date that the minor will be 21-years-old. This eliminates the need to calculate the guest's age from his or her birth date.

- **A genuine ID has specific features.** Make sure it contains the proper text and images and a correct license number. It should also contain a proper photo and the appropriate information on the back side. Use an ID checking guide when necessary.

- **Verify that the ID belongs to the guest.** Always compare the guest to the photo and the physical characteristics listed on the ID.

- **Follow the proper procedure for checking IDs.** Greet the guest and then ask him or her to remove the ID from his or her wallet. Be sure to look at both sides of it. Then, verify the ID. Always seek further verification if you think it's necessary. You can do this by asking for a second ID, comparing the guest's signature to the ID signature, or asking specific questions about information found on the ID.

- **Refuse service to a minor in the correct way.** Be firm, but express regret. Never sound authoritative or judgmental, and don't embarrass the person. You might say something like, "I'm sorry, but it's illegal to serve a minor."

- **Technology can help you identify fake IDs.** ID readers, UV lights, and magnifiers can all help you identify fakes. If you use an ID reader, make sure you compare the display with the actual information listed on the ID. Do not rely solely on the ID reader. ID readers should be used in addition to the other checking procedures identified in this chapter.

- **Take the correct steps if you spot a fake ID.** This includes refusing service or entry to your establishment. It might also include confiscating the ID. Always follow your company policy.

MULTIPLE-CHOICE STUDY QUESTIONS

1. **Which form of ID is acceptable for verifying a guest's age?**
   A. School ID
   B. Passport
   C. Birth certificate
   D. Voter registration card

2. **Which feature is an indication that an ID is valid?**
   A. A birth date
   B. Pictures of "locks"
   C. The word "authentic"
   D. A photo with raised edges

3. **Which feature is used by states to indicate that an ID belongs to a minor?**
   A. Placing the words "Secure," "Genuine," or "Valid" on the ID
   B. Issuing the ID in a vertical format
   C. Removing the minor's signature from the ID
   D. Placing pictures of "keys" on the ID

4. **Which is a good reason to reject an ID?**
   A. It has a bar code on it.
   B. A state seal can be seen under ultraviolet (UV) light.
   C. There is a ghost photo on the ID.
   D. The back of the ID is blank.

5. **What should you do to verify that an ID belongs to the guest?**
   A. Check for splits in the lamination.
   B. Verify the state seal is in the proper location.
   C. Compare the guest to the physical characteristics listed on the ID.
   D. Check the license number to see if the coding matches the personal information.

6. **Today is March 8, 2009. Based on these birth dates, which guest is old enough to drink?**
   A. March 7, 1988
   B. March 9, 1988
   C. April 10, 1988
   D. November 1, 1988

For answers, please turn to page 3-21.

ANSWERS

Page	Activity

3-2 Test Your Knowledge
1. False
2. False
3. True
4. True
5. True

3-3 Spot the Minor
All of them are minors.

3-6 Valid or Invalid?
ID #1 is not valid because it is missing a signature.
ID #3 is not valid because it has expired.

3-6 List the Features
1. It must contain the owner's birth date.
2. It must be current.
3. It must contain the owner's photo.
4. It must be intact.
5. It must contain the owner's signature.

3-8 To Serve or Not to Serve?
1, 2

3-11 Check It Out!
1. It should be digitized with 1D and 2D bar codes on the back.
2. It should contain the words, "THE BLUEGRASS STATE," which will be visible under UV light.
3. It should contain a repeating security feature of a stylized "K" within a box and the words "KENTUCKY TRANSPORTATION CABINET."
4. It should contain microprinting.
5. It should contain a license number with nine characters. It begins with a letter (generally the first initial of the last name) followed by the two-digit year in which the license was originally issued, ending with six randomly assigned digits. The license number is hyphenated in three groups.

3-15 Spot the Fake
Both ID #1 and ID #3 are fakes. ID #1 has the word "authentic" on it, while the word "secure" and pictures of locks can be seen on ID #3.

Continued on next page...

ANSWERS *continued*

Page	Activity

3-17 Rate the Response

1. Rating: 1—Effective

   Here is how the server handled the situation effectively:

   - He was not authoritative when refusing service.
   - He quoted the law and the consequences to both himself and the establishment when denying service.
   - He was firm in the decision to refuse service.

2. Rating: 1—Effective

   Here is how the valet handled the situation effectively:

   - He communicated important information to the doorman who was checking IDs.

   Here is how the doorman handled the situation effectively:

   - He thoroughly examined the ID to ensure it was genuine.
   - Since he was unsure if the ID belonged to the guest, he asked appropriate questions to verify it, including asking to compare the guest's signature with the signature on the ID.
   - He was polite when refusing entry.

3. Rating: 2—Ineffective

   The bartender made the following mistakes:

   - The bartender failed to use an ID checking guide to examine the out-of-state ID.
   - The bartender failed to notice that the photo did not match the guest. This should have prompted a more thorough examination of the ID.
   - The bartender failed to notice that the back of the ID was blank, indicating it was a fake.

4. Rating: 2—Ineffective

   The doorman made the following mistake:

   - The doorman failed to compare the readouts on the ID reader with the information on the IDs.

5. Rating: 2—Ineffective

   The bartender made the following mistakes:

   - The bartender failed to notice that the guest appeared nervous.
   - The bartender failed to ask the guest to remove his ID from his wallet.

3-19 Multiple-Choice Study Questions

1. B
2. A
3. B
4. D
5. C
6. A

Handling Difficult Situations

After completing this chapter, you should be able to:

- Identify the procedure for stopping alcohol service to a guest.
- Identify the procedure for handling intoxicated guests who attempt to leave the premises.
- Identify the procedure for handling a guest who has arrived at the establishment intoxicated.
- Identify the procedure for handling designated drivers.
- Identify the procedure for handling potentially violent situations.
- Identify the procedure for handling illegal activities.
- Identify the procedure that servers should follow if asked to perform an illegal activity.
- Identify incidents that require documentation.

TEST YOUR KNOWLEDGE

1. **True or False:** When stopping alcohol service to a guest, the backup person should stand as close to the guest as possible. *(See page 4-3.)*

2. **True or False:** Using statements such as, "You've had enough," when stopping service will deflect blame from you and defuse the situation. *(See page 4-3.)*

3. **True or False:** You should call the police if an intoxicated guest insists on driving away from the establishment. *(See page 4-9.)*

4. **True or False:** Guests can be served to the point of intoxication if they are traveling with a designated driver. *(See page 4-11.)*

5. **True or False:** You should physically restrain a violent guest so he or she does not cause injury. *(See page 4-12.)*

For answers, please turn to page 4-20.

INTRODUCTION

From time to time you may face situations that are difficult to handle. Your personal safety must always come first. If you feel threatened or you think you're in danger, remove yourself from the situation. Then notify a manager or the owner.

HANDLING INTOXICATED GUESTS

Despite your best efforts, guests may still become intoxicated. How you handle these situations is very important. It starts with the decision to stop service.

Stopping Service to Intoxicated Guests

You must stop serving alcohol to guests if:

■ They show physical or behavioral signs of intoxication.

■ You are concerned about the number of drinks they have had.

Some establishments allow employees to stop service but require them to notify management. Other establishments require management to stop service. Talk to your manager about your company policy on stopping service.

When stopping service to a guest:

1. Alert a backup. The backup person must be:

- Prepared to help.

- Close enough to observe.

- Not too close so as to appear threatening.

2. Enlist the help of other guests (if possible).

- Wait until the intoxicated guest steps away.

- Ask the guest's companion to help stop service. A friend or relative may be able to convince the guest not to order another drink. He or she may also be able to smooth over the situation.

3. Wait until the guest orders the next round before stopping service. Telling a guest that you're stopping service as you serve a final drink can upset the person. It also allows time for resentment to build. If you notice that a guest is becoming intoxicated you must stop service immediately. In some areas, you may be required to stop service while guests are still drinking their unfinished drinks.

4. Tell the guest you are stopping service. Always keep the conversation private. To prevent a confrontation:

- **Don't be judgmental.** Never use "You" statements, such as, "You've had enough." These sound judgmental and may offend the guest. Using statements like the ones listed below will help deflect blame from the guest and you. They will also help defuse the situation. Practice them until they become natural to you.

Say things like:

- *"Our company policy doesn't allow me to serve you any more alcohol."*

- *"I'm not able to serve you any more alcohol this evening."*

- *"We would be responsible if something were to happen."*

- *"It is against the law for me to serve you any more alcohol."*

Always alert a backup before stopping service.

Ask an accompanying friend or relative to help you stop service to a guest.

Express concern and empathy when stopping service to a guest.

When stopping service to a guest, offer nonalcoholic alternatives.

Express concern and be genuine. Tell the guest that you are concerned about his or her safety.

Say things like:

- ☐ *"I just want to make sure you get home OK."*

- ☐ *"We want you to come back again."*

- ☐ *"Why don't we call it a night? We'll see you tomorrow."*

Express empathy. Show the guest you understand how he or she is feeling. Make sure that you maintain eye contact while you talk to the guest, and nod and shake your head when appropriate. This will show that you are listening.

Say things like:

- ☐ *"I know this is frustrating or annoying, but I am concerned about your safety."*

- ☐ *"I know you're upset. I would be upset too, but we just want to make sure that nothing happens to you."*

- ☐ *"I'm sorry I can't serve you. Let me call you a cab so you get home safely."*

Be firm. Guests will often try to persuade you to change your mind or ask for "just one more" drink. Once you have made the decision to stop service, stick to it. Be patient and remain calm. Simply and clearly repeat your decision to stop alcohol service as often as necessary.

5. **Offer nonalcoholic alternatives.** Offer the guest coffee, soft drinks, or other nonalcoholic alternatives.

- This will allow time for the guest's body to process the alcohol he or she has consumed.

- If the guest came into the establishment with friends, it will also allow him or her to still feel like a part of the group.

You may stop service to a guest, only to find that the person is still getting drinks from companions. Immediately stop service to all of the guests and remove the alcohol from the table.

Stopping Service to Regulars

Occasionally, you may need to stop service to a "regular." This can sometimes be awkward, especially when the guest has been coming to the establishment for a long time. Never let this get in the way of doing the right thing! When guests have had enough, they have had enough, regardless of their patronage. Let your relationship work to your advantage. Express the genuine concern you have for their safety, but be firm.

HOW THIS RELATES TO ME...

What is your company policy for stopping service to a guest?

_____

_____

_____

SOMETHING TO THINK ABOUT...

A bride and groom spent the night in jail after the newlyweds were arrested on the way home from their wedding reception. The new husband was charged with driving while intoxicated. Officials said that the wife became belligerent after her husband's arrest and was then charged with public intoxication. She spent the night in jail in her wedding dress. A bartender at the reception said that he had noticed that the groom was slurring his speech while ordering drinks, but that he was afraid to stop service because he didn't want to ruin the couple's special day.

APPLY YOUR KNOWLEDGE: *Did They Handle It the Right Way?*

Read the scenarios and decide if the situations were handled correctly.

1. One of the guests at the bar, a tall and athletic man, had begun making rude comments and using foul language. Bill, a bartender, decided it was time to stop service. He asked another bartender to serve as his backup. When the guest asked Bill for another drink, both Bill and the other bartender walked over to the guest and stood in front of him. Bill told the guest that he was not able to serve him any more alcohol that evening. When the guest became angry, Bill told him that he would serve him one more drink, but that it would have to be his last. The guest told Bill he was leaving after that drink anyway. So Bill served him a final drink.

   Did Bill handle the situation the right way? Why or why not?

   _____

   _____

   _____

   _____

   _____

   _____

2. Maria, a server, was becoming concerned about two women that she had served a bottle of wine earlier. She overheard them say that they were going to order another bottle. When they had arrived, they had been quiet and reserved. Now they were loud and overly friendly with other guests. Maria talked to her manager, who agreed with Maria's decision to stop service and to back her up. As the women asked Maria for another bottle, the manager watched from across the room. Maria apologized and told the guests that her company policy would not allow her to serve them more alcohol. The women became outraged and insisted that Maria get another bottle. Maria said that she understood their frustration. She told them that she just wanted to make sure they got home safely. She then offered to bring them coffee.

   Did Maria handle the situation the right way? Why or why not?

   _____

   _____

   _____

   _____

   _____

For answers, please turn to page 4-20.

APPLY YOUR KNOWLEDGE: *Am I Saying That Right?*

Write *Yes* next to the statement if you think it is appropriate when stopping service to a guest or *No* if it is not.

1. _____ "I'm sorry, but I don't feel comfortable serving you another drink. How about a soda or a cup of coffee instead?"

2. _____ "This is the last drink I can serve you this evening."

3. _____ "We feel you've had enough, and it's against our policy to serve you any more alcohol."

4. _____ "I'm sorry, but I could get fired if I serve you another drink."

5. _____ "I think you've had enough, sir."

6. _____ "I'm not sure you can make it home, so I really can't serve you another drink."

7. _____ "You're not getting another drink because I think you're intoxicated."

8. _____ "I guess I can serve you another beer, but this will have to be the last one."

9. _____ "Sir, I am going to have to stop serving your friend. Can you make that drink your last drink and see that he gets home safely?"

10. ____ "I'm sorry, but it is against the law for me to serve you any more alcohol."

For answers, please turn to page 4-20.

For answers, please turn to page 4-20.

HOW THIS RELATES TO ME...

List statements you have used that have been successful when stopping service to a guest.

_____

_____

_____

_____

_____

SOMETHING TO THINK ABOUT...

Alex, a regular at Walker's Steakhouse, sat at the restaurant's bar. He had been there for hours having several drinks and a few light appetizers. In the last hour, Alex switched from drinking Manhattans to beer and double shots of whiskey. As he became increasingly loud, using foul language and slurring his speech, Marlon, the bartender, became concerned. Marlon knew that Alex was a valued customer and a friend of the owner, so he decided to inform his general manager about the situation.

Chris, the general manager, consulted with the restaurant's owner. Neither of them wanted to stop service because Alex brought a lot of business to the establishment. Instead, they decided to follow Alex home, since he lived close by. Chris agreed to use his car to follow Alex home.

Chris drove closely behind Alex, keeping Alex's car in sight. Just as they both safely made it through an intersection, however, Alex swerved and swiped the side of a parked car. He continued on his way without even noticing what he had done.

What do you think of the decision to follow Alex home? What should have been done differently?

SOMETHING TO THINK ABOUT...

Bar hopping is an important issue to keep in mind when serving alcohol. In a recent case, a man was killed when his truck collided with a vehicle speeding in the wrong direction. That vehicle was driven by an intoxicated man who had been drinking at four different bars that evening with a friend.

In another case, a woman was killed and her two-year-old daughter was severely injured when their car was hit by a drunk driver who had moved from bar to bar over a period of eight hours. By the time he had begun driving home, the man had consumed over 15 drinks at three establishments.

Handling Intoxicated Guests Attempting to Leave the Premises*

Once you've stopped service to a guest, the next step is to make sure the person gets home safely. This can be challenging when the guest has driven to your establishment alone. Whatever you do, never use physical force to try to stop the guest from driving.

Follow these steps to prevent an intoxicated guest from driving:

1. Try to convince the guest not to drive.

- Avoid being judgmental.
- Express concern.

2. Ask for the guest's keys. If the guest will not provide them:

- Warn the guest that you will call the police.
- Call the police if the guest insists on driving. Provide the police with the make, model, license plate number, and direction in which the guest was driving.

3. Arrange alternate transportation. This might include:

- Asking a sober companion to drive.
- Calling the guest's friend or relative.
- Calling a cab.

You should never "throw out" intoxicated guests, even if they are disturbing other guests or causing a scene. If you must ask guests to leave, arrange transportation for them.

The conversation you have with the guest throughout this process might go something like this: *"I'm sorry, but I'm not able to serve you any more alcohol this evening. I'd like to call someone to come and pick you up. If you decide to drive, I'll have no choice but to call the police. What would you like me to do?"*

*Always follow company policy when handling these situations.

_____

_____

Dealing with Guests Who Arrive Intoxicated

Sometimes, a guest might arrive at your establishment intoxicated. You always have the right to refuse service, but you should make sure the person gets home safely.

Take the following steps if guests arrive intoxicated:

If guests are intoxicated when they arrive at the establishment, try to refuse entry.

■ **Try to refuse entry.**

■ **Make sure the guests are not served alcohol if they enter the establishment.** Communicate with all appropriate coworkers about the guests' condition.

■ **Ask the guests for their keys.**

      If they refuse, tell them that you will call the police if they attempt to drive.

      If they insist on driving, call the police.

■ **If the guests have agreed not to drive, find alternate transportation.**

_____

_____

Designated Drivers

Many communities offer a designated-driver program. In this program, one person in a group of drinkers agrees to be the designated driver. The designated driver agrees not to drink alcohol during his or her visit. The establishment usually offers the person free food or nonalcoholic beverages. Sometimes the designated driver receives coupons for future visits.

Many guests think they will be allowed to drink to the point of intoxication if they have a designated driver. That's simply not true. You are still liable for overserving guests even if they have a designated driver. Let guests know that you will not overserve them despite having a designated driver.

Follow these steps when working with a designated driver:

■ Encourage the person not to drink alcohol.

■ If the person starts drinking, watch him or her like you would any other guest.

■ If the person does not drink, follow your company policy regarding the service of free items.

SOMETHING TO THINK ABOUT...

A 21-year-old designated driver was charged with driving under the influence after he sideswiped a telephone pole and flattened a brick mailbox. The youth was dropping off his third passenger after having dropped off two others in the early morning hours. He was reported to have had a blood alcohol content of .147.

A 35-year-old man was sentenced to two years in prison after killing a cab driver. The man had started drinking shortly after he had decided to be the designated driver for a group of friends. He had a blood alcohol content that was twice the legal limit. His four passengers were also seriously injured in the accident.

HANDLING POTENTIALLY VIOLENT SITUATIONS

You may face situations that could become violent. This might include guests who are rowdy or who are acting inappropriately. It might also include threatening or abusive behavior. You could even be faced with assaults or fights in the establishment.

In most states, if you are faced with these situations you must:

■ Make a reasonable effort to anticipate problems.

■ Prevent injuries.

To prevent injuries when handling potentially violent situations:

■ **Notify your manager.**

■ Pay close attention to guests so you will be aware of potential problems.

■ Involve your manager early to determine the best way to handle the situation.

■ **Call the police.**

■ Call the police whenever your safety or the safety of others is at risk.

■ Do not assume that the situation will resolve itself. It usually won't.

■ **Separate guests from the situation.**

■ This will help prevent them from being injured.

■ Never touch or try to physically restrain a violent guest.

HOW THIS RELATES TO ME...

How does your establishment require you to handle potentially violent situations?

_____

_____

_____

HANDLING ILLEGAL ACTIVITIES

It's against the law to allow certain activities to continue on the premises. That includes gambling, prostitution, and the possession or sale of drugs. When faced with these situations, you should do the following:

- **Consider your safety and the safety of your guests before taking action.**

- **Notify your manager.** He or she will decide what should be done.

- **Call the police.**

HOW THIS RELATES TO ME...

How does your establishment handle illegal activities?

_____

_____

_____

SOMETHING TO THINK ABOUT...

On a busy Friday night at Barry's BBQ, Quinn, one of the restaurant's bartenders, took a quick break. He stepped outside for some air. In the parking lot behind the establishment, Quinn noticed a young couple, a blonde woman and a dark-haired man, hunched over the hood of a car. They appeared to be taking turns at something. Quinn couldn't quite see what they were doing, but he thought it might be drugs. He hurried inside to get back to the bar, but since he wasn't sure about what he saw in the parking lot, Quinn decided not to say anything to his manager.

About an hour later, Quinn noticed the woman from the parking lot again, this time seated at the end of bar. She was talking loudly and acting aggressively toward another patron, Tim—a frequent diner at the restaurant. Her companion stood nearby and was also visibly angry. Quinn knew that Tim was a quiet guy who had never been involved in a confrontation at the restaurant. He watched in horror as Tim, who tried to back away from the couple, was tackled to the floor by the man, while the woman began to kick Tim's midsection and head.

Though the fight was stopped and the couple was arrested, Tim suffered severe injuries. Toxicology tests revealed that there were traces of cocaine in the bloodstreams of the couple at the time of the assault.

What should Quinn have done differently?

Management Support

You should always involve a manager when handling the situations discussed in this chapter, such as stopping service to a guest. There may be times, however, when the manager may not agree with your decision and may ask you to respond differently. If this happens, remember that you are liable for your actions while serving alcohol.

If you are not comfortable with what your manager has asked you to do, you should:

- **Express your concern.**

- **Ask the manager to do it instead.**

- **Talk to the owner or your human resources department.** This is especially important if you feel that you are being asked to do something that is against the law, such as continuing to serve visibly intoxicated guests.

APPLY YOUR KNOWLEDGE: *Rate the Response*

This activity requires Video/DVD 5: *Evaluating Real-World Scenarios.*
After watching each scenario from section 3 of this video, use the
rating scale below to rate how well the employee handled each
situation by placing the appropriate number in the space provided.

Rating scale
1 = Employee handled the situation effectively.
2 = Employee handled the situation somewhat effectively.
3 = Employee handled the situation ineffectively.

Video Segment	Description	Rating
1	Male guest entering an establishment	
2	Two female guests dining in a fine-dining restaurant	
3	Valet interacting with a guest leaving the establishment	
4	Two male guests watching a football game at a bar	
5	Female guest talking with a bartender at the bar	
6	Regular interacting with a bartender at the bar	
7	Guest talking to a female server at the end of the bar	
8	Bartender interacting with a guest in the restroom	
9	Group of friends with a designated driver	
10	Server interacting with a softball team	

For answers, please turn to page 4-20.

APPLY YOUR KNOWLEDGE: *Put It into Practice*

Now it is time to put together everything you have learned by practicing how to handle a difficult situation.

1. Choose a partner. Together, create a realistic scenario in which an employee must handle a difficult situation with a guest.

2. Act out the scenario in front of the group, with one of you playing the employee and the other playing the guest. Draw on your experience, or on things you may have witnessed in an alcohol-service situation.

3. As an audience member, provide constructive feedback for the other scenarios presented. As a group, discuss how well the employee handled the situation.

DOCUMENTING INCIDENTS

When an incident occurs on the premises, your establishment may require you to complete an incident report. An incident report is used to document what happened during the incident and what actions were taken. These reports help your organization determine if policies are effective or whether they need to be revised.

When filling out an incident report:

- Provide accurate information.

- Fill out the report immediately so important facts are not forgotten.

- Follow your company policy on what to include and how to document the incident.

Incident reports should be completed when:

- Alcohol service has been stopped to a guest.

- Alternate transportation has been arranged for a guest.

- A guest's ID has been confiscated.

- An illegal activity or violent situation has occurred.

- A guest has become ill.

SUMMARY

Here are some of the most important points from this chapter.

■ **You must follow specific steps when stopping service to a guest.** Begin by alerting a backup. Whenever possible, enlist the help of a guest's companions. Wait until the guest orders another round before refusing service. Keep the conversation as private and calm as possible. Avoid being judgmental, but be firm. Be empathetic and express concern. Finally, offer the guest nonalcoholic alternatives.

■ **Ensure intoxicated guests get home safely.** Ask an accompanying friend or relative to drive the person home. If the guest is alone, try to convince him or her not to drive, and ask for car keys. If the guest gives them to you, find alternate transportation. If a guest insists on driving, warn him or her that you will call the police. Do it if the guest persists. Whatever you do, never use physical force to try to stop a guest from driving.

■ **You might have to deal with guests who are intoxicated when they arrive at your establishment.** Try to refuse entry. If they enter, make sure they aren't served any alcohol. Ask these guests for their car keys. If they refuse, warn them you'll call the police and then do it if they insist on driving. If a guest has agreed not to drive, find alternate transportation.

■ **You can't overserve guests, even if they have a designated driver.** If a group of guests has a designated driver, let them know that you will not overserve them despite having a designated driver. Encourage the person not to drink. If the designated driver starts drinking, watch the person like you would any other guest.

■ **Follow the right steps when handling a potentially violent situation.** To prevent injury, you should anticipate problems and notify your manager before the situation becomes violent. If you are caught by surprise and violence is likely to occur, call the police. Try to separate other guests from the situation. Never touch or attempt to physically restrain a guest.

■ **It's against the law to allow certain activities to continue on the premises.** That includes gambling, prostitution, and the possession or sale of drugs. Notify your manager, and call the police.

■ **You might not always be comfortable with what your manager has asked you to do when handling difficult situations.** Express your concern to the manager. Ask the manager to do it instead. If necessary, talk to the owner or your human resources department.

■ **Complete an incident report when an incident occurs on the premises.** The incident report documents what happened and the actions that were taken. Ask your manager about your company's policy regarding incident reporting.

MULTIPLE-CHOICE STUDY QUESTIONS

1. **When stopping service to a guest, you should**
   A. tell the guest that he or she has had enough.
   B. ask the guest's companion to help you stop service.
   C. have a backup person stand next to you as you tell the guest.
   D. give the guest another drink if it will prevent a confrontation.

2. **Which statement should be avoided when stopping service to a guest?**
   A. "You've had enough."
   B. "I just want to make sure you get home OK."
   C. "It's against the law for me to serve you any more alcohol."
   D. "Our company policy does not allow me to serve you any more alcohol."

3. **To prevent an intoxicated guest from driving, you should**
   A. have the guest's car towed.
   B. warn the guest that you will call the police.
   C. physically stop the guest from getting into the car.
   D. physically stop the guest from leaving the establishment.

4. **If a guest is intoxicated when arriving at the establishment,**
   A. ask the guest to leave.
   B. physically restrain the guest.
   C. forcibly take the guest's car keys.
   D. refuse entry to the establishment.

5. **Which statement about designated drivers is true?**
   A. Overserving a guest who came with a designated driver is illegal.
   B. A server is not liable for overserving guests with a designated driver.
   C. Establishments are not liable for overserving guests with a designated driver.
   D. A guest can be allowed to become intoxicated if accompanied by a designated driver.

Continued on next page...

MULTIPLE-CHOICE STUDY QUESTIONS
continued

6. **If a fight occurs, you should**
   A. separate other guests from the situation.
   B. wait and see if the situation resolves itself.
   C. stand between the guests who are fighting.
   D. try to physically restrain the guests who are fighting.

7. **Which situation requires you to fill out an incident report?**
   A. A guest stumbles when getting out of his chair.
   B. A guest complains about the strength of his first drink.
   C. A guest has presented a fake ID, which was confiscated.
   D. A guest is rude to a server after waiting too long for a drink.

8. **You have decided to stop alcohol service to a group of guests, but your manager has told you to continue serving them. You should**
   A. serve the guests.
   B. ask the manager to serve the guests.
   C. tell the guests to leave immediately.
   D. express your concern but serve the guests anyway.

9. **When handling a fight, when should you call the police?**
   A. After separating the guests who are fighting
   B. After calming down the guests who are fighting
   C. After physically restraining the guests who are fighting
   D. As soon as your safety or the safety of guests is at risk

10. **You witness a drug transaction on the premises. You should**
    A. call the police.
    B. ignore the situation to prevent a possible confrontation.
    C. do nothing if the transaction occurred outside the building.
    D. warn the offenders that you are going to inform your manager.

For answers, please turn to page 4-22.

ANSWERS

Page   Activity

4-2   Test Your Knowledge

1.   False   2.   False   3.   True   4.   False   5.   False

4-6   Did They Handle It the Right Way?

1.   Bill did not handle the situation the right way. It was good that he asked the other bartender to be his backup. However, the backup should not have stood in front of the guest. A backup must be close enough to observe the situation but not so close so as to appear threatening. Once Bill made the decision to stop service, he should not have changed his mind. He should have held firm and repeated his decision to stop service. Then he should have offered nonalcoholic alternatives.

2.   Maria handled the situation correctly. She alerted her manager and used him as a backup. As a backup, the manager did well to observe from across the room. Maria was careful not to be judgmental when she stopped service to the guests. She expressed both concern and empathy. She was also firm in her decision to stop service. Finally, she offered the guests a nonalcoholic alternative.

4-7   Am I Saying That Right?

1.   Yes. The statement is phrased as an "I" statement and is not judgmental, which helps deflect blame from the guest. It also offers the guest a nonalcoholic alternative.

2.   No. Service is being stopped to the guest as the last drink is being served. It's best to wait until the guest orders the next round before telling him or her that you are stopping service.

3.   No. This statement is judgmental. It would be better to leave it at, "It's against our policy to serve you any more alcohol."

4.   Yes. The statement is phrased as an "I" statement and is not judgmental.

5.   No. This statement is judgmental and is likely to provoke a confrontation.

6.   No. While this statement sounds as though the person is expressing concern, it is actually judgmental. It would be better to say something like, "I want to make sure you get home safely, so I am not able to serve you."

7.   No. This statement is definitely judgmental and could provoke an incident.

8.   No. It sounds as though the guest has convinced the bartender or server to serve another drink after the decision was made to stop service. You must be firm and not change your mind once the decision has been made to stop service.

9.   Yes. You should always try to enlist the help of an accompanying guest when stopping service.

10.   Yes. The statement is phrased as an "I" statement and is not judgmental. It is appropriate to quote the law when stopping service.

4-15   Rate the Response

1.   Rating: 1—Effective

Here is how the hostess, the server, and the manager handled the situation effectively:

■   The hostess correctly informed the server about the signs of intoxication exhibited by the guest.

■   The server asked the hostess to alert the manager about the situation.

■   The server's statements were not judgmental when refusing alcohol service to the guest. He was also empathetic.

■   The server quoted the law when denying service.

■   The hostess called the police.

■   The hostess and server moved other guests away from the situation when the guest became violent.

■   The manager intervened when the guest became violent.

Continued on next page...

ANSWERS *continued*

Page	Activity

2. Rating: 1—Effective

   Here is how the server, the bus person, and the maitre d' handled the situation effectively:

   - The bus person alerted the server that her guests were exhibiting signs of intoxication.
   - The server alerted the maitre d' as a backup.
   - The server was not judgmental when informing the guest of her decision to stop service.
   - The server deflected blame from the guest to company policy.
   - The server expressed concern when stopping service.
   - The server was firm in her decision about stopping service.
   - The maitre d' was close enough to observe but did not appear threatening to the guests.

3. Rating: 1—Effective

   Here is how the valet handled the situation effectively:

   - The valet was firm but not judgmental.
   - The valet was empathetic and expressed concern for the guest's safety.
   - The valet threatened to call the police when the guest insisted on driving.
   - The valet arranged for alternate transportation.

4. Rating: 3—Ineffective

   The bartender made the following mistakes:

   - The bartender failed to inform the manager about the potential of a fight before it occurred, even though there were definite signs that the situation was escalating.
   - The bartender failed to call the police when the guests began fighting.
   - The bartender separated the two fighting guests and physically restrained one of them. The bartender also restrained a guest from leaving the establishment.
   - The bartender failed to separate other guests from the situation.

5. Rating: 3—Ineffective

   The bartender made the following mistakes:

   - The bartender used judgmental, disrespectful statements when stopping service.
   - The bartender did not attempt to stop the intoxicated woman from leaving the establishment.

6. Rating: 2—Somewhat effective

   Here is why the bartender was only somewhat effective:

   - The bartender's statements when attempting to stop service were not judgmental.
   - The bartender was empathetic and expressed concern.
   - The bartender offered the guest nonalcoholic alternatives.
   - The bartender did not, however, stick with the decision to stop service. Serving alcohol to an intoxicated guest is illegal.

Continued on next page...

ANSWERS *continued*

Page	Activity

7. Rating: 2—Somewhat effective

Here is why the server and the bartender were only somewhat effective:

- Their initial statements when stopping service were judgmental.
- The bartender tried to recover by deflecting blame for stopping service to the potential loss of the establishment's liquor license and being fired.
- The bartender asked how the intoxicated guest was getting home. It is unclear whether or not his companions were sober.

8. Rating: 2—Somewhat effective

Here is why the bartender and the manager were only somewhat effective:

- The bartender was effective because she reported the activity.
- The manager, however, failed to act on the information and did not call the police.

9. Rating: 3—Ineffective

The server made the following mistake:

- The server overserved the guests. Whether or not a designated driver is present, it is illegal to serve an intoxicated guest.

10. Rating: 2—Somewhat effective

Here is why the server was only somewhat effective:

- Once the server decided to stop service, the server did not secure a backup.
- The server initially was not judgmental when stopping service to the guest and then became judgmental after being insulted.
- The server expressed concern for the guest's safety.
- The server was firm in her decision to stop service.
- Once the server found out the intoxicated guest was receiving drinks from his companions, she stopped alcohol service and all alcohol was removed from the table. She could have put herself in danger, because she had no backup.

4-18 Multiple-Choice Study Questions

1. B
2. A
3. B
4. D
5. A
6. A
7. C
8. B
9. D
10. A

NOTES

Index

absorption, 2-3, 2-5, 2-6
age, 1-8, 2-6
alcohol content (*see* drink strength)
alcoholic beverage commission (*see* liquor
    authority)

BAC (*see* blood alcohol content)
backup, 4-3
bar tab, 2-12
bartender (*see* serving alcohol)
beer, 2-8
birth certificate, 3-5
blood alcohol content (BAC)
    calculation of, 2-10, 2-11
    definition, 2-2
    estimation chart, 2-11 *(exhibit)*
    factors affecting, 2-5, 2-6
    legal limit, 2-3, 2-10
body fat, 2-5
body size, 2-5
bus staff, 2-17

carbohydrate 2-19
carbonation, 2-6
carding (*see* identification)
citation, 1-6
civil liability (*see* liability)
communication by employees, 2-16, 4-10
counting drinks, 2-8, 2-9, 2-12
criminal charge, 1-4
criminal liability (*see* liability)

deep-fried food, 2-19
dehydration, 2-19
designated driver, 4-11
discrimination, 1-6, 1-9
documenting incidents (*see* incident
    report)
dram shop laws, 1-2, 1-4
drink promotions, 1-9
drink strength, 2-5, 2-8 *(exhibit),* 2-9
driver's license
    acceptable ID, 3-4 *(exhibit)*
    out-of-state, 3-4

driving while intoxicated
    prevention of, 4-9, 4-10
drugs, illegal, 4-13

emotional state, 2-6

fake ID (*see* identification)
fine, 1-4, 1-7
food, 2-6, 2-19

gambling, 4-13
gender, 2-5
greeter, 2-17
guest check, 2-12

happy hour (*see* drink promotions)
hosts and hostesses, 2-17
hours of service, 1-9
human resources department, 4-14

ID checking guide, 3-2, 3-8 *(exhibit)*
ID reader, 3-2, 3-16

identification (ID)
    acceptable forms of, 3-4 *(exhibit)*
    birth date, 3-5, 3-8
    characteristics of
        bar code, 3-10, 3-16
        ghost photo image, 3-2, 3-9
        hologram, 3-2, 3-9
        lamination, 3-2, 3-5, 3-10
        license number, 3-10
        magnetic stripe, 3-10, 3-16
        microprinting, 3-9
        optical variable device (OVD),
            3-9
        photo, 3-10, 3-12
        UV features, 3-9
    fake, 3-9, 3-16
    genuine, 3-8, 3-9, 3-10
    minor, 3-7 *(exhibit)*
    procedure for checking, 3-14, 3-15
    unacceptable forms of, 3-5
        (exhibit)
    validity of, 3-5 *(exhibit)*
    verification of, 3-5, 3-7 thru 3-13
illegal activity, 4-13
immigration card, 3-4
incident report, 4-16
inexperienced drinkers, 2-15
inhibitions, relaxed, 2-13
intoxicated guests
    driving, 4-9, 4-10
    laws, 1-9
    stopping service, 4-2, 4-3, 4-4, 4-5
intoxication
    assessment of, 2-8
    blood alcohol content, 2-3, 2-10,
        2-11
    monitoring by staff, 2-16, 2-17
    prevention of, 2-19
    stopping service, 4-2, 4-3, 4-4, 4-5
    refusing entry, 4-10
    signs of, 2-13, 2-14
    tolerance, 2-15

judgment, impaired, 2-14

lawsuit, 1-2, 1-4
legal age, 1-8, 3-8
    calendar, 3-8
liability
    civil liability, 1-2, 1-4
    criminal liability, 1-2, 1-4
liquor, 2-8, 2-9
liquor authority, 1-2, 1-6
liquor control commission (*see* liquor
    authority)
liquor license, 1-6, 1-7
liver, 2-2, 2-5

management, 4-14
medications, 2-6
military ID, 3-4 *(exhibit)*
minors
criminal liability, 1-4, 3-3
    identification of, 3-3 *(exhibit)*, 3-7,
        3-8, 3-12, 3-13
    refusing service, 3-3, 3-15
mixed drink, 2-9
motor coordination, 2-14
mouth, 2-3
municipality, 1-2
muscle, 2-5

nonalcoholic alternatives, 4-4

observation by employees, 2-16, 2-17
overpouring, 2-19

passport, 3-4 *(exhibit)*
photo *(see* identification)
police, 4-9, 4-10, 4-12
pregnant guests, 1-9
proof, 2-2, 2-8, 2-9
prostitution, 4-13

reaction time, 2-14
refusing entry, 4-10
refusing service, 3-15, 4-10
regular patron, 2-15, 4-5

salty food, 2-19
school ID, 3-5 *(exhibit)*
security staff, 2-17
serving alcohol
    civil liability, 1-2, 1-4
    criminal liability, 1-2, 1-4
    drink promotions, 1-9
hours of service, 1-9
legal age, 1-8
legal responsibilities, 1-3, 1-4
refusing service, 3-15, 4-10
small intestine, 2-2, 2-3, 2-19
standard measures, 2-8
state ID card, 3-4 *(exhibit)*
state law
    acceptable ID, 3-4 *(exhibit)*
    blood alcohol content, 2-3
    drink promotions, 1-9
    legal age, 1-8
    liability, 1-4
    liquor authority, 1-2, 1-6
    selling to minors, 1-4, 1-8
    unacceptable ID, 3-5 *(exhibit)*
stomach, 2-3
stopping service, 4-2 thru 4-5, 4-9

tolerance, 2-2, 2-15
transportation, alternate, 4-9

underage drinking *(see* minors)

valets, 2-16
violent situations, 4-12
voter's registration card, 3-5 *(exhibit)*

water, 2-19
wine, 2-8

Credits & Acknowledgements

Unless otherwise noted, all photography was done for exclusive use in this publication by Steve Garrett (Garrett Photography) or Ron Molk (Classic Images).

All photographs or images are presented for educational purposes only and should not be considered actual materials or settings.

No photographs in this publication may be reproduced without prior written permission of the publisher.

Requests to use or reproduce photos or images from this publication should be directed to:

Copyright Permissions
National Restaurant Association
175 West Jackson Boulevard, Suite 1500
Chicago, Il 60604-2814
Email: permissions@restaurant.org

Page	Description	Source/Credit	Status	Image #	Photographer	Notes
1-4	handcuffs	Getty Images	royalty free	AA022797	Siede Preis	
2-6	champagne	Getty Images	royalty free	FD001233	PhotoLink	
2-9	whiskey	Getty Images	royalty free	FD000067	John A. Rizzo	
2-11	BAC charts	Markham, M. R., Miller, W. R. & Arciniega, L (1993) BACCus 2.01: Computer software for quantifying alcoholic consumption. Behavior Research Methods, Instruments, & Computers, 25, 420-421.				
2-19	pizza	Getty Images	royalty free	FD001332	PhotoLink	
3-4	Utah license	2009 I.D. Checking Guide	courtesy of The Driver's License Guide Company	n/a	unknown	photo-edited
3-6	Georgia license	2009 I.D. Checking Guide	courtesy of The Driver's License Guide Company	n/a	unknown	photo-edited
3-9	Rhode Island license	2009 I.D. Checking Guide	courtesy of The Driver's License Guide Company	n/a	unknown	photo-edited
3-11	Kentucky page	2009 I.D. Checking Guide	courtesy of The Driver's License Guide Company	n/a	unknown	
Cover	martini with lemon twist	Getty Images	royalty free	FD000064	John A. Rizzo	
	martini with onion	Getty Images	royalty free	FD000065		
	bartender	exclusive image	exclusive image	DSC_0438	Alfred Rasho, Roxie Media Corporation	composited image
	ID checker (waist up)	exclusive image	exclusive image	DSC_0548		
	ID checker (waist down)	exclusive image	exclusive image	DSC_0659		
	bar and patrons	BananaStock	royalty free	23006849	Bananastock	